Mo

Mo

D0462691

Help Us Keep This Guide Up to Date

Every effort has been made by the author and editors to make this guide as accurate and useful as possible. However, many things can change after a guide is published—trails are rerouted, regulations change, facilities come under new management, and so forth.

We appreciate hearing from you concerning your experiences with this guide and how you feel it could be improved and kept up to date. While we may not be able to respond to all comments and suggestions, we'll take them to heart, and we'll also make certain to share them with the author. Please send your comments and suggestions to the following address:

Globe Pequot Press
Reader Response/Editorial Department
246 Goose Lane, Suite 200
Guilford, CT 06437

Or you may e-mail us at:

editorial@falcon.com

Thanks for your input, and happy trails!

Mountain Biking
Moab Pocket Guide

More than 40 of the Area's
Greatest Off-Road Bicycle Rides

Third Edition

David Crowell

FALCONGUIDES

GUILFORD, CONNECTICUT
HELENA, MONTANA
AN IMPRINT OF ROWMAN & LITTLEFIELD

FALCONGUIDES®

An imprint of Rowman & Littlefield
Falcon, FalconGuides, and Outfit Your Mind are registered trademarks
of Rowman & Littlefield.

Distributed by NATIONAL BOOK NETWORK

Copyright © 2014 by Rowman & Littlefield
Maps © Rowman & Littlefield

British Library Cataloguing-in-Publication Information available

ISSN 1545-9756
ISBN 978-0-7627-9327-3 (paperback)

∞™ The paper used in this publication meets the minimum
requirements of American National Standard for Information
Sciences—Permanence of Paper for Printed Library Materials, ANSI/
NISO Z39.48-1992.

The author and Globe Pequot assume no liability for
accidents happening to, or injuries sustained by, readers
who engage in the activities described in this book.

Contents

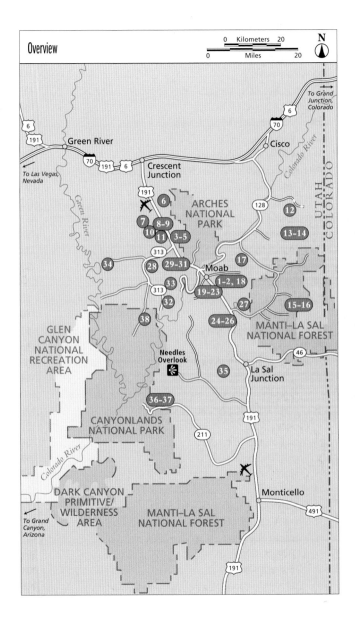

Acknowledgments

Where to begin? This would not have been possible without Will Harmon, my first editor, and Ann Seifert, Lynn Zelem, and Katie Benoit for wrangling this update, which is almost entirely a new book.

The town of Moab took me in and shared its energy. It's a special, spiritual place. Moab's bike shops and their personnel kept me up and running through more than 1,000 miles of desert pounding. A lot has changed since I penned the first edition of this book. Even the book's name has changed. Yet Moab's welcoming, fun-loving soul remains the same.

Jay Stocks, I was honored to be part of your family. Amanda and Stephen were an unexpected joy! Thanks to you and Tanya for making the latest update a pleasant and warm experience.

Thank you to Trail Mix and all the volunteers that help make Moab's trails the best in the world. And the folks that name those trails. And the folks that make it possible for them to do what they do.

Judd Freeman—it's always been good to ride with you. Having you as a friend is even better. Good luck with Rapid Cycling. I can't imagine anyone better to have a bike shop. I hope St. George appreciates what they have in you.

I also thank:

- All the riders past and present that blazed the way and continue to explore.

- Trail Mix, Moab Trail Alliance, Moab Trail Foundation, the Grand County Community Sand Flats Team, and the International Mountain Biking Association.

- Larry, Ned, Jennifer, Donovan and Monika, Patrick, Anthony, Chip, Rhonda, Rene, Lisa, Harry, Chase,

Heather, Timothy, Judy Pentz, Harris the Cozmic Hitchhiker, T'uellan, Mike, Christie McNeil, Dan, Joe Hendrickson, and everyone else who listened to me babble from my barstool.

- Eddie and Audrey Snyder and the White Rim crew: Lisa, Lisa, Dennis, Donna, Steve, Honga, Corinne, and Angela.

- The radio personalities Christie Williams, Keith Simpson, the vinyl dinosaur, Scotty-O, Tim, and Bon Kelly—from KZMU's dilapidated trailer days.

- Eddie McStiff's for taking me in, Mondo's for keeping me awake, and KZMU for letting me be a DJ.

- My brother, Clint, for the morale boost after 500 miles of desert heat and the unconditional support.

- My mom for letting me watch the house and "finish" the book, and my dad for calling me there and keeping me sane.

- Scott Adams, Dave Montgomery, Ron George, Chad Niehous, and Glen Casamassa for their help with this update.

- My son, Dawson, who at 10 weeks old visited his first two national parks during the second edition update and rode with me at 10 years old for this update.

- My daughter, Amber, who at 7 years old rode her bike with 12-inch tires on the Agate trail to help with this update.

- My wife, Heidi.

- The Earth Mother for giving me a place to play, laugh, and love.

Get Ready to CRANK!

Welcome, pilgrims, to the promised land. The land of standing rock, the *Toom'pin wunear Tuweap*. For seasoned riders and neophytes alike, this is where all trails eventually lead. This is the landscape our bikes were made for.

If Moab is the mecca for mountain biking, the reason is slickrock. Here, huge beds of ancient sandstone have been carved by wind and water into a maze of canyons, plateaus, pillars, and walls. Slickrock, however, is anything but slick. Tires cling to the sandstone like paint to canvas, encouraging amazing feats of fat-tire artistry. Riding here will improve your skills and open your mind to new possibilities.

Sculpted by nature, the land surrounding Moab provides a plethora of places to pedal. Mesa tops, canyon floors and rims, and the passes between cover environments ranging from open desert to old-growth juniper forests. The riding surface is just as varied. A single ride may roll over slickrock sandstone, ledgy bedrock, mud, cobblestones, and sand.

While the Slickrock Trail may be the point to the pilgrimage, sandstone snacks are offered throughout the region. But rock candy is only one entree of the region's menu to feed your mountain-biking soul.

The Manti-La Sals serve up singletrack as rugged as the riders who call Moab home. These old volcanoes never erupted, but their trails stoke a primitive mountaineering fire. Rocky, remote, and steep, they offer a cool alternative to the desert playground below.

Recent attention by Moab to the tastes of modern mountain bikers allows all riders to dine on a buffet of fast, flowing singletrack through the desertscape without choking on ATV or Jeep dust.

As you worship this holiest of mountain-biking lands, keep in mind that, as rugged as they may look, some surfaces were not created to bear the brunt of tires. Cryptobiotic crust, a living topsoil, can be destroyed by just one errant tire. And some of the hard-packed roads turn to gumbo when wet. With so many fat-tire enthusiasts coming to Moab, we must all tread lightly. Read the section on the desert environment titled "Riding Right!" and be an educated rider. Stay on the trail.

Your pilgrimage to Moab will be rewarded. Services are held daily here, and they're a blast!

Welcome to the promised land.

The Journey

The journey of 1,000 miles begins with the first turn of the cranks.

Many who make the pilgrimage to Moab do so with their own vehicles. From the south there is only one real route choice: US 191. From the north there are two choices: US 191 or UT 128.

From the west, travelers eastbound on I-70 should take exit 182 at Crescent Junction, which is 17 miles past the roadside town of Green River. From the east, travelers westbound on the interstate have a more scenic option. The second Cisco exit, exit 204, is for UT 128. This is known locally as the River Road because it parallels the Colorado River and skirts huge sandstone cliffs before joining US 191 just north of Moab. This road also features the Bureau of Land Management's Colorado Riverway campsites, Matrimony Spring, and a junction with the La Sal Loop Road.

From Denver drive west on I-70 for 6 or 7 hours to exit 204 or exit 182 and follow the above directions.

From Salt Lake City drive south on I-15 past Provo. Get off at exit 261 after passing Springerville and continue south on US 89, which leads to Thistle. Soon after take US 6 south past Price and Wellington, where it becomes US

191. Follow US 191 into Green River and onto I-70. Go east to exit 204 and then drop south on US 191 into Moab.

If your journey to Moab begins by air, Canyonlands Field offers service from Denver. The airport is 19 miles north of Moab on US 191.

Other air options include flying into Salt Lake City, Utah (236 road miles to Moab), or Grand Junction, Colorado (110 miles). Shuttle services are available from both these locations, as are rental vehicles.

Moab

In the beginning there was Moab. Lo verily this was good. It came to pass that others cast doubt as to whether this ground was worthy of the pilgrimage. Where, they asked, is the sacred singletrack?

Perhaps these troubled pilgrims had forsaken the dashes upon the rock. Perhaps they had grown weary of competing with big, steel beasts that shared the rugged roads. Or perhaps they yielded to temptation and bit off a hunk of the forbidden Fruita.

Whatever the cause, the keepers of the sacred land didn't flee. They reached for rake and shovel. They lobbied the powers that be. They toiled with ropes and moved mountains ... er ... well ... they moved some pretty big rocks.

Now, Moab boasts an ever-growing menu of mountain-bike specific singletrack: Klondike Bluffs, Moab Brands, Intrepid, Sovereign, Captain Ahab . . . the ever-expanding list goes on.

Moab is a great town. It is full of people who are friendly and nonjudgmental. It's hard to imagine that there was a time when the unwashed bikers had worn thin their welcome. Now, mountain bikes are big business.

Probably your first stop in town is the Moab Information Center. Located at Main and Center Streets, this is an excellent place to get oriented. They have maps, books, museum-like displays, and an informative staff with links to all the land-management agencies. Campground avail-ability and the weather forecast are posted here. A message board stands between the visitor center and Eddie McStiff's like a forgotten tribute to how the biking tribe passed messages before the smartphone era. Speaking of modern technology: The visitor center has free Wi-Fi.

You'll also likely need to stop by the old watering hole. No, not the saloon, though you *can* drink in Utah. You'll need a place to fill up your hydration bladders. Moab's got ya' covered with the Lions Park Transit Hub on the corner of US 191 and UT 128. City Park on 100 West and 400 North also has some water spigots, and, of course, the bike shops (appendix H) can fill you up.

If you really are looking for an Old West way to fill up, about 0.1 mile down UT 128 from Lions Park is Matrimony Spring. This spring is often crowded and has been the subject of some controversy. The spring has been unofficially open for, well, forever. It was unofficially maintained by good folks. It reached a point where folks suspected that it was being contaminated somewhere upstream as it wasn't passing the stringent state standards. It was capped and rerouted to drain to the river. There was a lot of angst, and then it was unofficially open again. It used to be a must-do part of the Moab experience. Now? Well, the water is there, still coming out of the rock.

While no longer the water-oriented plague it once was, dust-caked campers in need of showers can still be spotted zombie-walking the streets of Moab. Appendix D lists where to wash off.

Moab has embraced the bike tourist and caters to every need. This includes food, coffee, rooms, showers, rental jeeps, Laundromats—everything a big city could boast, at mostly reasonable prices. Sure, it's cheaper to rent a four-by-four in Salt Lake City but then you're in Salt Lake City.

Food. You'll need food, right? If you're staying in town at a hotel, then you'll be eating out. There's a big city's worth of restaurant choices here. For the do-it-yourself folks, there are a couple of grocery stores on Main, a health-food store on 100 North, and there's always Dave's Corner Market at Mill Creek Drive and 400 East on the way up to Slickrock Trail (Ride 1).

With food and water needs met, what more could a pilgrim want? Culture? No longer is the choice limited to Muzak and religious programming. A wide variety of real music is played on Moab's own FM station, KZMU 90.1 and 106.7 Call in a request (435-259-5968) and it's a good bet it will be played. Want a bit of Moab while planning your trip? KZMU is also available online.

OK . . . food, water, culture. What? You didn't get enough adventure? You have a kid that still has too much energy? The town now has its own skate park located in the northeast side of City Park. It's open to bikes and boards.

Now it's all been covered. Oh, wait. Mountain bikers have been known to rehydrate with a beer or two after a ride. Justly or not, Utah is famous for its laws regarding alcohol. While it still has a variety of laws to regulate your alcohol consumption, significant revisions in 2009 have allowed the spirits to flow more freely. Flow is a relative term as liquor can be doled out only 1 ounce at a time. No doubles and only one drink at a time. If you're looking for alcohol to go, you'll need to hit the state-run liquor store for anything stiffer than 3.2 beer. It's at 55 W. 200 South, which is Utah-speak for "turn at the Pancake Haus. It's on the left. If you get to NAPA, you've passed it."

The basics of a desert pilgrimage are water, food, water, shelter, and water. Shelter hasn't been covered yet. Moab has a hotel/motel guest capacity of at least 1,800. That seems like a lot for a town this size. Heck, it certainly looks like enough during a tour down Main Street. But during the season it is very hard to find a room. Some annual events (I'm looking at you Jeep Jamboree) will take up all the rooms in town and many possibly in Green River.

Rooms run the gamut from budget to luxurious. Many of the high-end rooms are found in bed-and-breakfasts. Ask about bike-related rules. Most proprietors in this mountain-biking mecca are enlightened, but some establishments still have a few archaic practices. "Can I store my bike in my room?" is a good question to ask. Currently, crime isn't a big problem in Moab, and practicing normal bike security is usually enough. But you never know. Spring and fall are certainly the riskiest times. Recreational-vehicle campgrounds offer sites in and out of town. They have showers and tent camping available. Bureau of Land Management (BLM) and La Sal National Forest lands offer a couple of pay camping sites as well. (See appendix F.) The aforementioned Moab Information Center posts the current status of national park and forest service campgrounds.

Hopefully you won't need to know that the Moab Regional Hospital, located at 450 W. Williams Way, is open 24-7. The phone number is 911 for emergencies or (435) 719-3500.

Being Prepared

Mountain Biking Moab Pocket Guide is a where-to-ride book. How to ride is another story. What to bring lies in the gray area between the two subjects. Common sense is the rule here. Bring what makes you feel comfortable. If you need a personal mechanic to follow you, pay Cycle Sean to do so. If you like to ride in just shorts and a hat, well, it's your body. But here are a few ideas on equipment, tools, first aid, clothing, water, and weather.

Equipment

Back in the day, Moab ate up bikes. Now, with all the developments, it still does. Any piece of gear that was dreamed up for mountain biking probably had Moab in mind. A necessity is a small chainring or a climbing gear.

You can climb incredibly steep angles of slickrock if you've got a gear low enough for your legs to spin. If the biggest rear cog (gear) is 28 or smaller, then the small chainring on the front should be 22 or smaller. Modern bikes all have gearing that will get you up the steepest slickrock ascent. I've met folks at trailheads that didn't really understand how their gears worked. If this is you, well, you may want to check into that.

It's also important to have a way to carry lots of water. Two cages with large water bottles is the minimum. A back-borne hydration setup is ideal. If you'll be out on Slickrock Trail all day, both setups are a good idea.

Other equipment, like shocks, makes things nicer, but the gear ratio is most important. We rode this stuff "fully rigid" back in the day. It's still possible, but your body will be much happier the day after with a modern bike with suspension.

If you're riding a department-store bike and wondering why everything seems so hard to do, well, it's because you're riding a department-store bike and Moab ain't no department store. If you're stuck with very subpar equipment, you can still have fun. Hurrah Pass, Moab Canyon Pathway, Agate, and some of the easier Moab Brand trails come to mind. I mention this because some parents may have kids who want to ride and those kids may have subpar bikes. I'm not talking about old-school bikes. They are just as fun as they ever were.

The local bike shops (appendix H) have a range of rentals available to those who arrive sans bike or have discovered their own equipment is lacking.

Tools

Tools are a touchy subject for bikers—each has his or her own opinion. The riding here is torturous on equipment. Rock can peel the knobbies right off a tire and eat the derailleur for dessert. Keep one question in mind:

"What's the farthest I'd have to walk?" I weigh out the tools and my desire not to walk, which usually results in this list.

Sense of humor—perhaps the most important item

Spare tube—for the first flat

Patchkit—for additional flats

Tire Boot—for when the slickrock eats your tire

Air pump

Allen wrench

Channel locks—a moment of silence for the ultimate tool

Spare cables—a fancy long one with both brake and derailleur ends if you still have cable brakes

Chain tool—I secured a crank with one of these!

Pocket knife—Hey, this is a desert. Ever watch *Survivor?*

Duct tape—wrap a supply around the seat post—and bow down before it

Headlamp or flashlight—for the walk home after dark

If you can't replace a tube without tire levers, bring them too. You can always just bring $5 and hope it buys a repair from a passerby.

This list is minuscule for some and totally foreign to others. I've seen wonders done with nothing more than energy-bar wrappers. Just remember that cell service is fleeting in Canyon Country and, with time, everywhere is within walking distance.

First Aid

Consider packing a first-aid kit. The most important item to put in the kit weighs nothing: prevention. Remember that safety is your responsibility. Read up on desert hazards and know your biking limits. Then ask yourself, "How far will I be from help?" and pack accordingly. Help is more readily available than it used to be. The sheer number of bikers increases your chances of getting the word out that you need help. However, around Moab, help is often hindered by the very terrain that brings us here. You could notify someone of your problem and still be stuck overnight. Here is a partial list to consider:

- Butterfly-closure bandages
- Adhesive bandages
- Gauze compress pads and gauze wrap
- Allergy pills
- Emergency water-purification tablets
- Moleskin
- Antiseptic swabs
- Sunscreen
- Energy bar
- Emergency blanket
- Signal mirror
- Whistle

The best thing to bring is a riding partner. Riding alone in remote areas isn't wise. Cell service is usually unavailable. If you do have a bad crash or succumb to the heat, cold, lightning, wild animals, or act of God, remain calm and make decisions with a clear mind. Also remember the primary rule of first aid: Do no harm. This means doing only what you must to keep the injured person alive and as comfortable as possible until you can get to a doctor. With luck you may run into help on the way out (and a pox on those who don't offer help). The point is don't waste time and don't panic. Deal with things as they come up and keep going.

Always wear a helmet. Slickrock facials are no fun. But they are worse with a naked melon. I can tell you're a smart person because you're reading this book. Wear a helmet. Some other cycling apparel also makes sense from a first-aid standpoint. Gloves will save your hands from scrapes and cuts, and cycling shorts save your butt.

Hopefully you won't need to know that the Moab Regional Hospital, located at 450 W. Williams Way is open 24-7. The phone number is 911 for emergencies or (435) 719-3500.

Sun

The desert sun does more than just create a need for water. It can literally cook you!

Sunburn is easy to combat. Thirty minutes before going out, liberally apply a sunscreen of at least SPF 15 and reapply it frequently. Pay particular attention to your nose, cheekbones, ears, and the nape of your neck. Sun-sensitive riders will want to take more extreme measures to blot out the sun. Some experts suggest long-sleeved, loose-fitting, white clothing. Be sure your clothing doesn't lead to a second hazard, overheating. By the way, SPF 55 rocks.

Heat exhaustion is a prominent danger, especially in summer when temperatures above one hundred degrees Fahrenheit are common. Just being hydrated is not enough. Sometimes the body just can't keep up with rising temperatures, and its cooling system shuts down. Warning signs include pale skin, heavy sweating, nausea, weakness and dizziness, thirst, headache, and muscle cramps. If you experience any of these symptoms, find shade immediately and cool off as well as possible. Douse your head and chest with water (save some for drinking) and try to keep air moving over your skin. If you try to ride through heat exhaustion, you'll likely end up with heatstroke, a far more serious—and often fatal—condition.

Always wear sunglasses to protect your eyes from sun, eye strain, kamikaze insects, and flying rocks spun up by your tires. A helmet visor also helps and will keep your eyes on the trail and the sun off your nose.

Of course the best ammo is prevention. During summer in the canyon regions, plan to complete your ride by 9 a.m. The desert is intense. Show your respect. Check out the Ride Finder for some suggestions for good rides for the summer.

Water

A human's weight is at least 80 percent water. A desert is defined by a significant lack of water. This makes for a simple rule: Bring as much water as you can carry. Also drink lots of water before riding. Many people drink far too little water before heading out and are already dehydrated.

After you become an experienced desert rider, tailor how much fluid you bring on a ride. For now, however, bring all that can be carried. That means water-bottle cages filled with large bottles, in addition to your back-borne water bladder.

Odds are someone in your group will run out of water or start rationing. Share rather than ration. It's also a good idea to bring something to replenish electrolytes too. Use the back-borne bladder for water and the bottles for electrolyte drinks. And keep an extra gallon or two in the car for après-ride rehydration.

Of course, carrying lots of water does nothing if it's just along for the ride. A body in the desert is said to need more than a gallon of water a day. Add a bit of strenuous exercise and do the math. Drink lots and drink often.

Lungs dump huge amounts of moisture into exhaling breath, which, combined with sweating, quickly dehydrates the body. Don't run a quart low. Drink!

For information on water found on the trail, see the "Riding Right!" section later in this chapter.

Weather

Moab's weather can be as extreme as its landscape. But the biggest concern for bikers, besides the baking sun and broiling heat, are the sudden storms that sweep across the desert. Intense thunder-boomers bring deadly lightning, strong winds, and wash-filling rains. When thunderheads start forming, head to town and enjoy the local ambience.

If caught in a storm, some precautions can help keep you safe. Check how close the lightning is with the old trick of counting the seconds between the flash and the thunderclap. A count up to "five Mississippi" means the last flash was about 1 mile distant. If you hear thunder, it's possible to be struck, and it's time to take cover. When in the open, ditch your bike and other metal objects. Then find a place to hunker down. Don't be the tallest thing around, and do not hide under the lone tree. The idea is to reduce your contact with the ground and avoid being a lightning rod or hiding under one. Look for a depression or low point and crouch (don't lie down). Try to avoid puddles and moving water. It's easy to feel exposed in Canyon Country, but don't panic.

If you duck into a dry wash or canyon to avoid lightning, be alert for flash floods. Flash floods in the desert are beautiful events. Instant rivers shoot off of slickrock cliffs, carving their paths just a bit deeper. But these same waters are downright ugly when you're in their path. The key is awareness. A flood can sweep through even when it's not raining in your area. Water can travel far in a desert down twisting washes. Listen to the radio for flash-flood warnings, and heed them. If caught in a flood, don't try to outrun it. Get out of the wash to higher ground and wait. Enjoy its beauty and don't tempt fate.

Rain can also turn local soils into a sticky glop that is a cross between marshmallow crème and B-movie swamp slime. It's slicker than snot and gloms on to anything it touches. The soils northwest of town seem to be worse than elsewhere after a rain. Rides 3 to 7, 13, 23, 34, and 35 should be avoided during and immediately following rain. The rain does make the sand easier to ride! Riding after a storm is great for Poison Spider (Ride 31) and the extremely sandy rides. But beware: Slickrock is temperamental when wet and can live up to its name.

Spring tends to bring a flurry of dramatic storms; summer storms are less frequent. Fall storms are less violent but usually colder.

When to Ride

The most common times to ride are spring and fall when throngs of riders pour in from across the globe. The big events coincide with this migration pattern. Spring sees the 24 Hours of Moab, and fall brings Outerbike (outerbike.com) and the Moab Ho-Down Mountain Bike Festival and Film Festival (moabhodown.chilebikes.com). Keep in mind that other forms of recreation tend to enjoy the same spring-fall pattern. Things like the Jeep Jamboree can make rooms and campsites scarce. This makes planning ahead a good idea.

The spring season tends to run from college break until the no-see-ums (annoying, biting flies) show up in late May. The trails are most crowded during this season.

Fall starts with the falling temperatures of mid-September and lasts as long as the weather stays nice.

Winter sees few riders, but the riding can be nice. Although snow can and does occur, many days bring calm air and a warm sun, making riding a treat. The upper mesas and mountains are snow covered, but the lowlands are usually rideable. Sandy trails firm up from frost, and the crowds are only a memory. Of course, patches of ice on slickrock and changing weather are factors to be reckoned with. In the past the town closed up shop in winter. Now you'll find a full range of services and possibly even some off-season discounts.

Summer is also a time of fewer riders. The few who have ridden here in July know why. Temperatures above one hundred degrees cook bikers as they search for shade. Any shade. To ride in the summer requires early starts (dawn's early light) and completing rides by 9 a.m. Some people ride in the evening, but so many factors make that dangerous that it's not recommended. If you do venture out after dark, however, a strong light with a full charge, an extra bulb, and an extra battery is a good idea . . . along with a full moon. If you're in Moab during summer, try riding in the La Sals. Temperatures there range in the low eighties and the terrain is awesome. Nights are cool, just right for camping.

Appendix E is a list of average temperatures to help you plan your riding season. Of course, as with all averages, anything can and does happen.

Riding Right!

The desert ecosystem is very fragile. Sure it seems rugged as it tears apart high-dollar bike rigs and their riders. But the land is fragile at heart. The ways humans can damage an environment are unlimited, but keeping it safe requires only respect and knowledge.

The basic building block of the desert is cryptobiotic soil. This is a fancy word for living dirt. It's chock-full of nutrients that feed the plants and even holds the dirt in place. You don't need to know *how* it works. It just does. At any rate, this crusty dirt is breakable. Just riding or stepping on it destroys the organisms within, leaving a scar for at least a decade and probably harming the area for fifty years. Luckily it's just as easily protected. Don't ride off-trail, and if you walk off-trail, do so only on slickrock. Many people say they know what cryptobiotic soil looks like and can easily avoid it. The black, crusty castellations typical of one form are indeed easy to recognize, but these living soils also take many other forms that are virtually indiscernible from plain old dirt. If you walk off-trail in the desert, you are most likely damaging cryptobiotic soil.

The next slice of tiny life involves water. You may actually find water on the trail occasionally, but do not use it. First of all, the potholes that catch rainwater are very important to wildlife. That includes the tiny waterborne creatures that hatch, mate, and die all in the short life span of the pothole. Bikers filling water bottles kill these creatures. Secondly, sweat, skin oils, and bike by-products (such as lube) all change the chemical makeup of the water. Wildlife can't go fill up at a faucet when they get back to town. You can. Don't use their water except in an emergency. Don't ride through or dip into the potholes.

The nature of springs and seeps allows a bit more interaction. They are often rock-filtered and quite fresh. However, unless you know that a particular spring is safe, don't drink from it. Matrimony Spring on UT 128 is a popular watering hole, but it is unregulated.

If you find yourself in a situation where you need to use the available water, be forewarned. This region has a wealth of minerals that dissolve in surface and groundwater. The human body does not cope well with some minerals, particularly when they're poured down the gullet in copious quantities. Arsenic, to name one, is not an elixir of life. It can cause cancer over the long haul and is toxic in higher doses over the short run. Most portable water filters do not remove arsenic, lead, and other toxic minerals. If you must drink the water, limit your intake to the amount needed to get you back to civilization. Use a filter to remove bacteria and other gut-loving life. Springs are the best bet, but stay away from anything near mine tailings.

How to Use This Guide

In the beginning, mountain biking in Moab was mainly on four-by-four trails, many of which were constructed in the search for uranium. As biking boomed, the need for bike-specific trails led to the construction of trail networks. These newly constructed trails are extremely well blazed with most junctions signed with "you are here" maps.

Each ride section of this guide provides an overview of a trail or network, shows it on the map, and gives mile-by-mile directions for a commonly followed route. Network rides will have additional information to allow riders to make informed choices for exploring the network.

The aim is to inform you so your trail time is memorable for all the right reasons. Remember, the best trail in Moab is the one you're riding on!

Most of the information in this book is self-explanatory. But if anything in a ride description doesn't seem to make sense, reread the following explanation of our format.

The information is listed in an at-a-glance format. It is divided into twelve sections:

The **ride number** refers to where the ride falls in this guide. Use this number when cross-referencing between rides for an easy method of finding the descriptions. The ride name refers to the name of the trail. Where more than one name exists, one has been chosen that best reflects the nature of the trail.

Location tells, in general, where the ride is in relation to Moab.

Distance is the length of the ride or segment in miles.

Riding time is an estimate of how long it will take to complete the ride. It represents trail time and does not include stops. If the ride is rated more difficult or strenuous than what you usually ride, add some time to the estimate. If rated much higher, add a big chunk of time. The scenery and physical challenge of these rides warrant plenty of stopping. As you pedal through a few rides in this book, compare your ride times with those listed in the guide and adjust your estimates for future rides accordingly.

Physical difficulty estimates the physical challenge of the ride. The levels are easy, moderate, and strenuous. The following are descriptions of what went into the rating:

Easy: Rides are mostly flat, but this may include some rolling hills. Any climbs will be short. Easy rides around Moab are harder than what the locals may call easy in other places.

Moderate: Rides will have climbs; some may be steep. Strenuous sections may occur, but the majority of the ride is moderate. Even on a moderate ride, some steeper sections may force some cyclists to dismount and walk.

Strenuous: Rides put the granny gear to work! The steeps may be long, grueling tests of endurance, power, and determination.

Remember this region is tougher than most, and the ratings are for comparison between rides around Moab. Easy rides can still have you gulping air, and moderate ones may induce you to walk. Walking a bike is a perfectly legitimate way to transport it. Also remember that this guide is for everyone, from beginners to experts. Compare your first rides to the levels listed here to get a feel for the classifications. Also bear in mind that technical sections that exceed your ability will be tiring and can make an easy or moderate ride seem strenuous.

Technical difficulty is not a problem with your new anti–chain-suck device. It is a rating from easy to challenging that quantifies how much biking skill is needed to keep you in the saddle with the rubber side down. Specific reasons for the rating might be listed. These ratings may seem low when compared to other regions; Moab's terrain may be tougher than anywhere on the globe. What may be challenging in Alabama or Oregon could be moderate to challenging here.

Easy: Basic bike-riding skill needed for riding smooth and obstacle-free routes. No easy rides are in this guide. This is Moab!

Easy to moderate: Mostly smooth tread with minor difficulties. Ruts, loose gravel, or obstacles may exist, but they are easily avoided.

Moderate: Irregular tread with some rough sections, steeps, obstacles, gravel, sharp turns, slickrock, small ledge drops. These will have obvious route options or lines through them.

Moderate to challenging: Rough going! The tread is uneven with few smooth sections. The line is limited as it weaves through rocks (boulders, babyheads, basketballs), sand, eroded washes, downfall, slickrock snacks, bedrock ledges, and any combination of them all. These obstacles often occur on steeps!

Challenging: Continuously broken, rocky, or trenched tread with frequent, sudden, and severe changes in gradient. Slopes necessitating off-the-seat riding and a nearly continuous barrage of obstacles where the line is tough to find and unforgiving if missed.

Again these ratings are for comparison's sake. Extreme obstacles may exist on any trail, and in this dynamic environment riders should be ready for obstacles at all times. Gauge your ability against the scale after your first few rides to get a feel for the ratings, and remember that different obstacles require different techniques.

Trail surface describes what the tires ride on when they are rubber-side down.

Land status lists the land-management agency. The rides in this guide are mostly on public lands. Appendix C gives the information needed to contact the various land-management agencies about rules, regulations, permits, and updates.

Maps include USGS maps that show each ride's area. These maps can be used for a more detailed view though they may not show the ride's route. Each *Mountain Biking Moab* map and profile should be more than sufficient for navigational and planning purposes.

Finding the trailhead tells you, well, how to find the trailhead. In most cases the directions begin from the Moab Visitor Center at the corner of Center Street and Main. This will be listed with the initial description of network trails.

Navigation tips: Trail segments that are part of a network will have any information to aid in route finding listed in this section along with any pertinent GPS data.

The Ride lists where to go and how to find the way back. Attached to the descriptions are odometer readings. These are estimates. They provide a yardstick to measure against.

The **elevation profiles** provide a good look at what's in store by graphically showing altitude change, tread, and ratings. The ups and downs of the route are graphed on a grid of elevation (in feet, above sea level) and miles pedaled. Route surface conditions (see map legend) and technical levels are also shown on the graphs. The technical levels are rated as follows: 1, easy; 2, easy to moderate; 3, moderate; 4, moderate to challenging; 5, challenging. Pluses and minuses cover the in-between areas. These are frequently used to distinguish between the many high-difficulty rides.

Note that these graphs are compressed (squeezed)

to fit on the page. The actual slopes you will ride may not be as steep as the lines drawn on the graphs—it just feels that way. Also, some extremely short dips and climbs are too small to register on the graphs. All such abrupt changes in gradient are, however, mentioned in the mile-by-mile ride description.

The **maps** are clean, easy-to-use navigational tools. Closed trails are not usually shown but may be listed in the ride description. Painstaking effort has been taken to ensure accuracy. The nature of Canyon Country has led to these simplified maps. While each nook and cranny may not be depicted, sufficient terrain is shown to keep you on track.

This guide doesn't pretend to be omniscient. Ratings and ride accounts are as accurate as possible. However, everyone is different. Individual riders excel in different skills and have different tastes. Use the guide as a starting point. Though regulations, ownership, and even the land itself may change, this guide will help get you home in one piece. If you have an inadvertent adventure you want to share, drop me a line.

Ride Finder

Beginner's Luck
- **3.** Moab Brands: Bar-M, Rusty Spur, Lazy, EZ
- **6.** Klondike Bluffs: Agate, Jasper, Jurassic
- **11.** Monitor and Merrimac
- **28.** Gemini Bridges Area: Gemini Bridges

Singletrack Rides
- **3.** Moab Brands: North-40, Sidewinder, Bar-B, Lazy, EZ, Long Branch, Deadman's Ridge, Rusty Spur
- **4.** Klonzo Trails
- **5.** Sovereign Singletrack
- **6.** Klondike Bluffs: Dino-Flow, EKG, UFO, Alaska, Homer, Nome, and basically everything there
- **14.** Fisher Mesa
- **15.** Moonlight Meadow
- **16.** The Whole Enchilada
- **16.** Upper and Lower Porcupine Singletrack (The Whole Enchilada)
- **18.** Prospector
- **19.** Pipe Dream
- **22.** Amasa Back Network: Pot Hole Arch, Rockstacker, Captain Ahab, Jackson Trail
- **28.** Gemini Bridges Area: Bull Run, Arth's Corner, Getaway, Great Escape, Little Canyon Singletrack
- **28.** Magnificent-7
- **32.** Intrepid Trail System

Slickrock Playground
- **1.** The Slickrock Trail
- **3.** Moab Brands: Circle-O, Rockin'-A
- **7.** Hidden Canyon
- **8.** Tusher Canyon's Left Side
- **9.** Tusher Too—Tusher Canyon's Right Side
- **10.** Bartlett Wash

Technical Tests

1. The Slickrock Trail
3. Moab Brands: Deadman's Ridge, Long Branch, Killer B
6. Klondike Bluffs: EKG, UFO, Homer, Nome
16. Lower Porcupine Singletrack (The Whole Enchilada)
17. Porcupine Rim
19. Pipe Dream
22. Amasa Back Network: Rockstacker, Jackson Trail, Captain Ahab
31. Poison Spider Mesa and the Portal Trail

Notable Climbs

12. Top of the World
16. Burro Pass (The Whole Enchiulada)
20. Moab Rim
22. Amasa Back Network: Amasa Back (Classic Ride)
33. Jug Handle Loop—The Shafer Trail

Great Downhills—The Need for Speed

12. Top of the World (the return)
13. Onion Creek
15. Moonlight Meadow
16. The Whole Enchilada
16. Burro Pass (The Whole Enchilada)
16. Hazzard County (The Whole Enchilada)
17. Porcupine Rim

Epic Rides—A Day in the Saddle

1. The Slickrock Trail
16. The Whole Enchilada
23. Jackson Hole (Hurrah Pass Trails)
24. Behind the Rocks Trail
27. Flat Pass
28. Magnificent-7
30. Golden Spike
34. Hey Joe Green Loop

Trying to Avoid the Summer Heat

Map Legend

〜70〜	Interstate Highway	✈	Airport
〜191〜	US Highway	∩	Arch
〜128〜	State Highway	⌣	Bridge
FR-378	Forest Road	▲	Campground
	Local Road	▮	Gate
	Gravel Road	▲	Mountain/Peak
= = = = =	Unimproved/4x4 Road	P	Parking
▬▬▬▬▬	Featured Route	⌣	Pass
- - - - -	Trail/Singletrack	🛆	Picnic Area
• • • • •	Portage	■	Point of Interest/Structure
+—+—+—+	Railroad	👥	Restroom
•—•—•—•	Fence	🏠	Ranger Station
╪══╪══╪	Power Lines	⬭	Rock Formation
⊓⊓⊓⊓⊓	Cliff Edge	✕	Rockhounding Site
– – – –	State Border	×	Spot Elevation
〜	River/Creek	♂	Spring
⬭	Body of Water	♙	Tower
⠂⠂⠂⠂	Sand	○	Town
▦▦▦	Slickrock	❶	Trailhead
⌐ ⌐ ⌐	National Forest/Park/ Wilderness Area	◈	Viewpoint/Overlook
▭	State/County Park	❓	Visitor/Information Center
⌐ ⌐ ⌐	Miscellaneous Area		

1 The Slickrock Trail

This is the ride that made Moab. The mix of strenuous wall climbs and hair-raising dips, half-pipes, and ledge drops on unbelievably high-traction sandstone will make you a changed rider. This is *the* Slickrock Trail. The promised land. The point to the pilgrimage. It is also crowded. Riding it during high season means waiting above the drops for a wave of riders to climb up, then descending with your own wave. It means playing leapfrog with other groups as each struggles to climb, drop, and maneuver around the loop. For those not held by a necessity to color within the lines, crowds can be avoided by exploring the undashed rock. Either way the views and thrills are unparalleled. If the trail frightens you, well, good. The hazards are fairly visible and therefore avoidable (walkable). This description chooses the "easier," clockwise, path, which gains a big chunk of altitude on a steep pitch (aka Cogs to Spare), making this direction seem less strenuous. Either way sees each and every obstacle. The numerous spurs and unmarked rock offer days of fun and are left undescribed to allow self-discovery of the free-form playground that is slickrock. Simply avoid crushing crust or poisoning potholes. Enjoy!

Location: 3.6 miles east of Moab on Sand Flats Road

Distance: 10.5-mile lariat-shaped loop with the practice loop (9.7 miles without). Numerous spurs and free-form exploring can increase mileage dramatically.

Riding time: About 1.5 to 5 hours. This isn't a misprint. Riders in excellent shape can crank this out in 1.5 hours. Others play on the rock or miscalculate the time it takes to walk the steeps. Don't be caught in the dark on the rock.

Physical difficulty: Strenuous. Most of the short pitches are amazingly steep. Your bike has the traction to climb them if you have the strength and technique to power it.

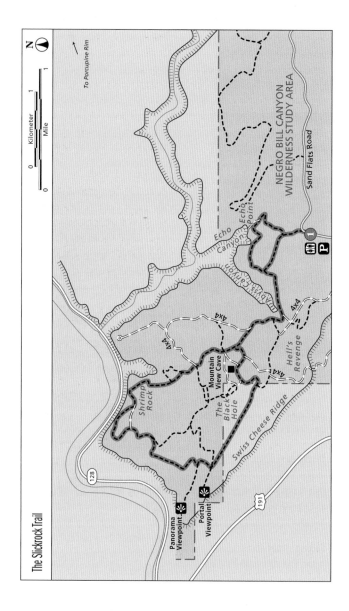

The Slickrock Trail

To Porcupine Rim

0   Kilometer   1

0   Mile   1

N

NEGRO BILL CANYON
WILDERNESS STUDY AREA

Sand Flats Road

Echo
Canyon

Echo
Point

Abyss Canyon

4X4

4X4

Hell's Revenge

4X4

4X4

Shrimp
Rock

Mountain
View Cave

The
Black
Hole

Swiss Cheese Ridge

Panorama
Viewpoint

Portal
Viewpoint

128

191

P

1

Technical difficulty: Challenging. The entire trail isn't one long trials maneuver, but any lapse of attention can mean a slickrock facial followed by a run to the emergency room. The technical spots are expert caliber with official danger sections marked with black diamonds in the painted dashes. Don't count on all the hazards being marked or described here.

Trail surface: 10.5 miles on slickrock. The geologically aware will get a laugh knowing that this rock is not of the actual Slick Rock formation of Entrada sandstone. With the exception of an occasional sandy wash, the entire trail is on Navajo sandstone. The route is marked with painted white dashes. Slickrock has come to mean any sandstone that holds bike tires like a pit bull holds a bone. In case you were wondering, the name "slickrock" comes from the fact that to shoed horses sandstone is slicker than snot on a glass doorknob.

Land status: BLM. The Community Sand Flats Team (435-259-2444) is doing a determined job of maintaining order in the area while nature repairs itself from past abuses. If you want to camp up here, check out appendix F.

Maps: USGS Moab; *Slickrock Trail Map* (free with access fee)

Finding the trailhead: From the Moab Visitor Center parking lot at Center Street and Main in Moab, turn right onto Center. Go 0.3 mile east on Center and turn right onto 400 East. Go 0.4 mile south on this wide road to Mill Creek Drive and turn left (Dave's Corner Market is on the corner). Go another 0.5 mile to a stop sign, then continue straight through the intersection onto Sand Flats Road. A cemetery is on the left. This road passes "America's most scenic dump" to reach the Sand Flats Recreational Area gate (see appendix G) in 1.8 miles. Pay the appropriate fee and continue 0.6 mile to the parking lot for the world's most famous bike trail. Total distance from downtown to the trailhead is 3.6 miles. GPS: N38 34.914' / W109 31.158'

The Ride

0.0   From the parking lot, head north to the well-marked trailhead. Odometer readings start at the mini–cattle guard gate.

0.2   This first hill foreshadows the ride's delights and arrives at the first decision point. Turn right onto the practice loop. It is no easier than the rest of the trail, but it offers a taste of slickrock for those without the time, strength, or desire to ride the entire trail. It also makes the trail longer for those who want more rock. A left here heads 0.8 mile to the junction described at 1.6 below. This description follows the practice loop first.

0.7   A spur goes right to Echo Point. Spurs are marked with white dots instead of dashes. Be careful when going to viewpoints! They tend to be located on very high cliffs that appear suddenly. (Odometer readings do not reflect side trips on spurs.)

1.6   The practice loop merges with the Main Trail. Keep right to continue or left to complete the practice loop and return to the trailhead. By now you've gauged your skills and fitness to make a good decision. It's 0.8 mile back to the trailhead. If you're ready, let's go right.

2.1   The Abyss viewpoint.

2.2   The dashes descend into a wash to what is probably the hairiest move so far: a rough, ledgy drop into a sandy gully immediately followed by a rock hop back onto the sandstone. Locals call this Wooly Gully. Oh, what fun it is! A spur leaves to the left just prior to the wash and heads to the Hell's Revenge Jeep Trail.

2.3   This sand trap precedes a spur to the left that cuts to the 3.7-mile point and accesses a sandy route beneath Swiss Cheese Ridge. To exit the trap requires a deft, technically challenging move and good line selection. Some riders' cheeks may hurt by now from all the grinning! There's plenty more ahead.

2.9   Join the main loop. "Easier" and "Harder" are painted on the rock at this intersection. This description opts for the clockwise—

easier—direction. See the ride's introduction and the elevation profile for why.

3.5 Mountain View Cave comes into sight (to the right) up on the rock. Then a spur to the Black Hole goes right.

3.7 The spur from mile 2.3 reenters on the left. Don't look now, but a rock wall blocks the path ahead. It's the hill mentioned in the ride introduction. To have any chance of climbing Cogs to Spare, hit the lower part with some speed and clean a grooved section of rock while nailing the granny gear. "All" that remains is the incredibly steep climb up to Swiss Cheese Ridge—most mortals will dismount and push this one. The top is a welcome level grade.

4.3 Before the main trail turns right and leaves Swiss Cheese Ridge, look left to see Moab, Moab Rim, Gold Bar Rim, and the Portal. The Portal is where the Colorado River crosses the Moab fault and heads into Canyonlands National Park. It is also where the famous and dangerous Portal Trail runs (see Ride 31). A spur continues ahead to the Portal Viewpoint.

4.35 Another spur goes right just after the first technical drop of the descent. It wanders past Upper Shrimp Rock and intersects with two other spurs.

4.4 The spur to Panorama Viewpoint darts left for some hair-raising vertical exposure.

4.7 Spin through a little sand to raise your appreciation for the smooth rock. A spur goes left to a cliff-side view of the Colorado River below Updraft Arch.

5.4 A spur heads right to the three-way intersection below Upper Shrimp Rock.

6.1 A spur cuts right to a point 0.3 mile short of Shrimp Rock.

6.6 Natural Selection Viewpoint. Be careful near the edge to keep your DNA in the genetic pool.

6.8 The spur from mile 6.1 enters on the right.

7.1 Shrimp Rock. This may be the heart of Moab's mountain-biking soul. Speak your favorite mantra and eat an energy bar to honor this holiest of rocks.

7.3 This steep, known as Stairway to Heavin', starts with a 3-foot rock hop.

7.6 This spur heads left to the Ice Box Canyon Viewpoint.

7.8 The Ice Box spur returns on the left.

7.9 Spurs head off right and left, marked by fake dinosaur tracks. Left is a sandy four-wheel-drive road, and right goes behind the Black Hole.

8.2 Drop down to some sand.

8.5 Back at the harder/easier junction. Go left to return to the trailhead.

9.8 Keep right for the direct route home. It's relatively level for 0.3 mile, then one last grunt. The Practice Loop leaves to the left here.

10.4 With the parking lot in sight, a sudden wheel-grabbing ditch sneaks up. "Matt's Mellon" lacks the telltale danger paint.

10.5 Trailhead.

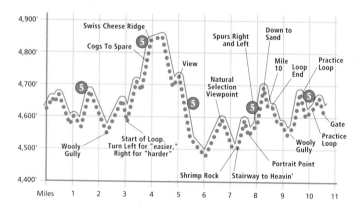

2 Moab Canyon Pathway and Lions Park Transit Hub

When you think of Moab, you don't think of bike paths. You picture slickrock, ledges, tight turns, rocks, and ribbons of singletrack. So what is a bike path doing in a book about mountain-biking Moab? What you don't think about—but should—is how you'll get around or how cars, bikes, and narrow roads will interact.

Moab thought about the problem, and the Moab Canyon Pathway is part of the solution. It runs 8.5 miles up from the Colorado River all the way up to UT 313. When completed it will wind along the river and UT 128 connecting the campgrounds and Porcupine Rim's exit point. Now campers can ride all the way to town without vehicular combat. Now folks can ride from town all the way to Moab Brands (Ride 3) and Gemini Bridges (Ride 28) without getting on the highway. This is a good thing.

Keep in mind that pedestrians and joggers use the trail. Most foot traffic is between town and Negro Bill Canyon. Be nice. They're just like bikers only without wheels. The Moab Canyon Pathway is also a boon for roadies seeking epic rides out to Dead Horse Point. Speaking of epic, the pathway can be used by those doing the Mag 7 trails around Gemini Bridges (Ride 28) as well as those returning to town from Porcupine Rim (Ride 17) and the Whole Enchilada (Ride 16). The whole path system is anchored by the Lions Park Transit Hub, where there is parking, shade, and restrooms.

Moab Canyon Pathway and Lions Park Transit Hub

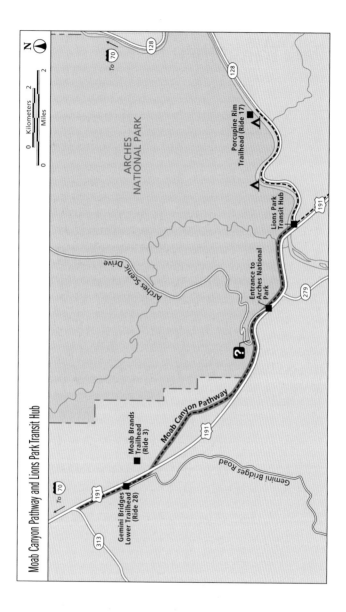

Location: Where US 191 and UT 128 meet, 2.5 miles north of downtown Moab

Distance: About 6.0 miles from the hub to Moab Brands

Riding time: 20 to 45 minutes to climb over 600 feet from the hub to the Moab Brands parking lot. The decent is much shorter.

Physical difficulty: Moderately easy. The path climbs almost 600 feet.

Technical difficulty: Easy

Trail surface: Asphalt that's as smooth as a baby's cheek

Land status: BLM and state land

Maps: USGS Merrimac Butte, Moab, and Gold Bar Canyon

Finding the trailhead: From the intersection of US 191 and UT 128, don't go anywhere. Look around you. The Lions Park Transit Hub is on the southeast corner. That's the start. The pathway can be picked up at the campgrounds upriver as well as the exit to Porcupine Rim (Ride 17). Another place to access the pathway is 0.7 mile north on US 191 on the right. In town you can access the path via your bike. GPS: N38 36.174' / W109 34.503'

The Ride

0.0 From Lions Park Transit Hub, cross the bridge and head northwards toward Arches National Park.

0.8 Alternate trailhead.

2.1 Be careful crossing the entrance road to Arches National Park.

4.0 Killer B, part of Moab Brands trail network, deposits riders here.

4.5 Sidewinder enters from the left.

4.8 Sidewinder enters again from the left.

5.2 Deadman's Ridge, part of Moab Brands trail network, deposits riders here.

5.4 Sidewinder leaves to the west and Escape enters from the east.

5.9 The southern end of Brand M trail joins here on the right (east).

6.9 Moab Brands parking lot is off to the right. This pathway turns westward and passes underneath US 191.

7.5 Pass by the end of Gemini Bridges Road (Ride 28).

8.7 Highway 333. A parking lot is on the north side of the highway. Return the way you came or enjoy some of the trails you passed by on the way back.

17.4 Arrive back at the Lions Park Transit Hub.

3 **Moab Brands Trail Network**

Connected to town with the Moab Canyon Pathway (Ride 2), Moab Brands network of trails offers up something for everyone without requiring a huge time commitment or even a long drive to the trailhead. If your group has varying abilities or you need a quick fix, this is a good bet. Part of what used to be the Courthouse Wash loop in the first two editions of this book, Moab Brands takes advantage of the maze of roads that cross the terrain between US 191 and Arches National Park. The Bar-M trail is described below. However, the beauty of this made-for-bikes playground is the ability to mix and match the trails to suit your cycling mood.

Oh, yeah. The "Brands," spell MOAB. Bar-M, Circle-O, Rockin'-A, Bar-B—MOAB, get it?

Starting at M they get harder up to B. Also note that Killer B and Bar-B are *not* the same.

Location: 10 miles north of Moab

Distance: The route described below is an 8.2-mile loop. You can choose longer or shorter rides.

Physical difficulty: Easy to strenuous

Technical difficulty: Easy to extremely challenging

Trail surface: Singletrack, slickrock, dirt road, sand, paved pathway

Land status: BLM and state land

Maps: USGS Merrimac Butte. Route maps are posted at most junctions.

Finding the trailhead: From Center Street and Main in Moab, head north 9.8 miles up US 191 and turn right. Follow the gravel road right and then left into the parking area. GPS: N38 39.111' / W109 40.099'

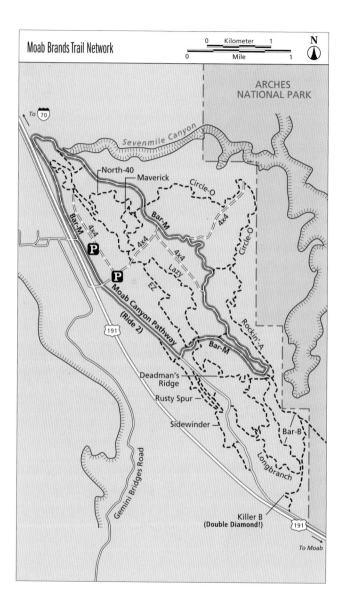

Moab Brands Trail Network

To 70

ARCHES NATIONAL PARK

Sevenmile Canyon

North-40
Maverick
Circle-O

Bar-M
4x4

4x4

Circle-O

P

P
4x4
Lazy

Moab Canyon Pathway
(Ride 2)

EZ

Rockin-A

Bar-M

Deadman's
Ridge

Rusty Spur

Sidewinder

Bar-B

Longbranch

Gemini Bridges Road

191

Killer B
(Double Diamond!)

191

To Moab

Kilometer
Mile

N

Bar-M

This loop can access most of the other options around here. As a multiuse trail, motorized vehicles such as motorcycles or ATVs can be seen here. Bar-M is a reasonable place for new riders who are trying to assess their off-road comfort levels. If you're comfortable, add Circle-O or Rockin'-A. Keep in mind that it's OK to walk up any hills. Don't forget to shift into the easier-to-pedal gears with both shifters.

Distance: 8.2-mile loop. This can be a long way for a new rider. An option at mile 3.6 allows one to cut the distance in half.

Physical difficulty: Moderately easy
Technical difficulty: Easy
Trail surface: Dirt with some rocky patches

The Ride

0.0 From the parking area backtrack on the road you drove in on.

0.2 Turn north at this junction with the Moab Canyon Pathway. You should still be following the road you drove in on. Those wishing to ride in a counterclockwise direction should turn south here. I've described a clockwise direction to access the other Brands in an order to spell out MOAB.

0.4 Leave the entrance road and continue straight. This was once the highway.

1.9 Keep an eye out for a right turn. It's well signed.

2.1 Keep right (south). North and east can continue to Klonzo and Sovereign trails (Rides 4 and 5). Also, just ahead is a short spur to overlook Sevenmile Canyon. Careful, that's a cliff.

2.4 Keep left. Right is an old road that leads down to a portion of North-40.

3.3 Junction with Circle-O trail. Bar-M continues straight ahead. West on Circle-O leads to the North-40 trail. East is the Circle-O trail, which eventually reconnects to the Bar-M or can join the Rockin'-A trail before again returning to the Bar-M.

3.6 Keep straight. The road that intersects from the right (west) heads straight back to the parking lot in 0.6 mile. Assess your fitness level and turn for home if you need to.

4.6 The Circle-O rejoins on the left. Continue on Bar-M by keeping right. Another option is to head east on Circle-O and then head southward on Rockin'-A to rejoin the Bar-M farther ahead.

6.0 Major intersection. The Bar-M turns back upon itself and heads for home. The Bar-B trail lies to the south. The Rockin'-A trail also has a junction here.

7.1 We've descended back to the Moab Canyon Pathway. A few roads crisscross here. Just keep heading downward and you'll get to the pathway. Turn right and follow the pathway toward the parking lot.

8.1 Turn right and follow the road into the parking lot.

8.2 Arrive back at the parking lot.

....

Circle-O

Circle-O takes you on slickrock. Slickrock isn't slick at all. In fact, it's like sandpaper and your tires cling tightly to it. This slickrock is fun for advanced riders, but Circle-O is a great place to introduce someone to ridin' the rock. It can be intimidating to new riders. Maybe picturing it as a wide, bumpy sidewalk would help? Keep your eyes out for wheel-grabbing grooves. When you go to cross a small, wheel-size dip in the rock, lift your front wheel to keep it from stopping. Stop and walk across if you're not ready for such a test.

Distance: 2.9 miles point to point
Physical difficulty: Moderate
Technical difficulty: Moderately easy
Trail surface: Slickrock
Navigation tips: A line painted on the rock shows you the way to go. Accessing Circle-O from the north via Bar-M is a good way to start out. (North junction with Bar-M trail: GPS N38 39.651' / W109 39.868'; south junction with Bar-M trail: GPS: N38 39.122' / W109 39.116')

....

Rockin'-A

The slickrock here is a step up in technical difficulty from Circle-O. Look out for some tight twists to keep on the trail. Check the section "Riding Right!" (see "Get Ready to CRANK!" in the introduction) to see why staying on the trail is so important in the desert.

Distance: 1.6 miles point to point
Physical difficulty: Moderate
Technical difficulty: Moderate
Trail surface: Slickrock
Navigation tips: A fun loop is Bar-B, Rockin'-A, Circle-O, and North-40 on home. The trail is marked on the Entrada sandstone with a stripe. (North junction with Bar-M trail GPS: N38 39.689' / W109 39.888'; south junction with Bar-M GPS: N38 39.127' / W109 39.106')

....

Bar-B

This is mostly singletrack but there is some slickrock. The trail works well counterclockwise. At the junctions with Killer B and Long Branch, it loops back, skirting the Arches National Park boundary on an abandoned road.

Distance: 2.2-mile loop
Physical difficulty: Moderate
Technical difficulty: Moderately challenging
Trail surface: Singletrack and some slickrock
Navigation tips: Links to Deadman's Ridge, Longbranch, and Killer B—all technically challenging trails. Trail joins Bar-M at GPS N38 38.271' / W109 38.487'.

Lazy

This is a good singletrack that flows through the desert. It works well as a moderately easy loop with the EZ trail. Lazy is intended to be a one-way trail from south to north.

Distance: 1.5 miles point to point
Physical difficulty: Moderately easy
Technical difficulty: Moderately easy
Trail surface: Singletrack with a couple rocky spots

Navigation tips: Riding Lazy is a good way to see if you're ready for this stuff. If you find your skills lacking, take the Bar-M to the Moab Canyon Pathway (Ride 2) for your return journey. The start is shared with the EZ endpoint at GPS N38 39.186' / W109 39.990'.

EZ

For beginners this isn't that "EZ," but more-seasoned riders will flow along this trail. Like most trails here, the tread can get soft in spots.

Distance: 1.25 miles point to point
Physical difficulty: Moderately easy
Technical difficulty: Moderately easy

Trail surface: Dirt singletrack with some rocky patches and sandy spots
Navigation tips: Is designed as the return portion of a loop with Lazy. As such, its start point is at the endpoint of Lazy. GPS: N38 39.186' / W109 39.990'

Rusty Spur

Rusty Spur is a good beginner ride, though new riders may even consider this a technically challenging ride with two scary cattle-guard crossings. Take the trail downward. After admiring the view from the sweeping left-hand turn, come back up the other side. The pathway awaits for an easier return. If things look dicey right off the bat, take the first opportunity to return to the pathway and find something more to your liking. Perhaps Bar-M?

Distance: 1.5 miles point to point
Physical difficulty: Easy
Technical difficulty: Moderately easy
Trail surface: Rusty-red dirt that will hopefully be packed for you

Navigation tips: Connects to the Moab Canyon Pathway in three places. GPS: N38 38.581' / W109 39.693'

North-40

This is a more technical loop with options to expand or shorten the experience. It is solid fun for anyone with a bit of dirt experience—a fun flow through the desert.

Distance: 4.0-mile loop
Physical difficulty: Moderate
Technical difficulty: Moderate
Trail surface: Dirt with some rocky patches
Navigation tips: The loop has junctions that allow you to modify it. It's also the quickest way to get to Circle-O. If you take the Maverick trail upward, you'll miss the connections to Circle-O. GPS: N38 39.186' / W109 39.990'

Sidewinder

This gives riders an option for a moderately technical descent rather than just rolling back to Moab on the path. It also has more climbing as well, so be warned. Sidewinder throws a bit of everything at you. Depending upon your skill set, you may think the moderate rating is being kind. There's a very steep spot, some edge riding that may feel exposed, slickrock, rock weaving, and a dry-wash entry and exit. Each of those things is moderately technical, which may add up to a challenging side dish.

Distance: 1.5 miles
Physical difficulty: Moderate
Technical difficulty: Moderate
Trail surface: Singletrack and slickrock

Navigation tips: The uppermost trailhead is near the terminus of Rusty Spur (GPS: N38 38.418' / W109 39.451'). Connects with Rusty Spur. An early escape route is available if Sidewinder's venom is too tough.

Deadman's Ridge

A full-on, gnarly trail. It hurts your lungs, tests your skills, and gets your heart pumping for many reasons. Deadman's ends at the Moab Canyon Pathway at the old highway's Deadman's curve (GPS: N38 38.038' / W109 38.911').

Distance: 3.1 miles point to point
Physical difficulty: Strenuous
Technical difficulty: Challenging
Trail surface: Singletrack and slickrock that is often busted up for your cycling pleasure

Navigation tips: If you want a longer trail, grab Long Branch. Though at this level, you're doin' fine just picking your own way around here. GPS at Bar-M: N38 38.573' / W109 39.278'.

Long Branch

Check out what I said about Deadman's Ridge and think, "even more so." The good news for most riders is that you can't accidentally get here without first having ridden Deadman's or Bar-B.

Distance: 1.0 mile
Physical difficulty: Strenuous
Technical difficulty: Challenging
Trail surface: Singletrack and slickrock served in momentum-halting hunks

Navigation tips: Taking Deadman's Ridge to Long Branch gets you to Killer B. If you don't want to be on Killer B, take Bar-B back to something a bit more sane. GPS: N38 37.845' / W109 38.612'

Killer B

There isn't any climbing to speak of, but you'd better have strength left because you'll need serious skills and big nerves for Killer B. Basically, there comes a point where you need to get your body way off your bike, put your seat in your chest or farther if you can, grit your teeth, and point down. Walking here is only a bit easier. I take that back: Walking with cleats and a bike may be worse. But be prepared to do so before turning down this trail. It's that steep.

Distance: 0.7 mile

Physical difficulty: Strenuous. I suppose hanging back over the rear of your bike can be strenuous. If it makes you think twice before riding this, all the better.

Technical difficulty: Extremely challenging

Trail surface: Loose, broken rock; insanely steep slickrock and singletrack

Navigation tips: Before the final drop there's a fork in the trail. Left leads to the old, closed portion of the trail. Stay right and finish the descent. You can be seen riding Killer B from US 191, though I don't think anyone would notice you lying on the ground. The ride deposits you at the bottom of the Moab Canyon Pathway (GPS: N38 37.203' / W109 38.285') for a nerve-calming ride back to town or up to the Moab Brands again. The trail starts at a junction with Bar-B (GPS: N38 37.615' / W109 38.160').

4 **Klonzo Trails**

This place is like a dream. You know, the one where suddenly you're on your mountain bike and you see singletrack before you that seems to go wherever you look. Are you following the trail or is it following you? It's like a flying dream, but you're awake. You're at the Klonzo Trails. There are hills here and technical challenges, but all seem perfectly placed. If you are an advanced rider, you may lament the lack of life-altering obstacles, except you'll be too busy smiling. I asked my 10-year-old son to review this trail. The ride was probably a bit above his ability level when we started. Here is what he wrote: "I think you should ride Kleko trail [we both had a hard time remembering the name . . . was it a dream?]. It is fairly easy [actually it's intermediate] and every trail marker you reach will have you saying, 'one more.' You can choose trails that are easy or harder depending on your biking skills. I rate this trail ***** [five stars]!!!!!"

Location: 12 miles north of Moab; 18.5 miles south of I-70

Distance: 8.5 miles of singletrack arranged so you can shorten or lengthen your ride

Riding time: 45 minutes

Physical difficulty: Moderate

Technical difficulty: Moderate

Trail surface: Packed dirt and slickrock

Land status: BLM

Maps: BLM trail map

Finding the trailhead: Drive north 12.8 miles from Center Street and Main on US 191. Turn right onto Willow Springs Road. Stay on Willow Springs Road for 2.8 miles to reach the trailhead on the left. At 1.6 miles down the road you'll have to cross Willow Creek, which is usually dry but often very sandy. If you don't have a strong SUV, you may wish to park closer to US 191 and ride to the trailhead. You'll also pass by the Sovereign trailhead 2 miles down the

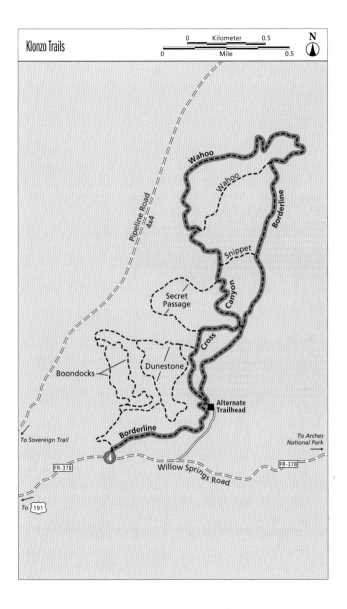

road. If you want to go directly to Klonzo from I-70, it's 18.5 miles to Willow Springs Road. Trailhead GPS: N38 42.133' / W109 39.137'

Borderline

As its name implies, Borderline runs up the eastern boundary of the area. It's a good way to gain altitude as you warm up for your Klonzo experience. It's a good, solid singletrack with just enough breaks in the climb to keep the dream alive.

Distance: 1.7 miles point to point from the lower lot to Wahoo
Physical difficulty: Moderate
Technical difficulty: Moderate
Trail surface: Packed singletrack and slickrock
Navigation tips: Borderline connects to Cross Canyon just above the upper parking lot then continues on to Snippet and Wahoo. Taking Cross Canyon over to the bottom of Wahoo then counterclockwise up is a fun way to the top (GPS: N 38 42.134' / W 109 39.130').

Wahoo

This is the uppermost trail in the area. On paper the loop looks like something from a string-theory presentation. In the real world it's a wonderful mix of slickrock and desert singletrack. The lower part of the loop is the suggested way to climb Wahoo. Its slope is gentle enough and the slickrock steps low enough to make climbing fun. Did I just say "fun" and "climb" in the same sentence? Yup. After you complete the climb, you'll flow right through the boulders over dirt and slickrock. If you giggle inside and yell, "Wahoo!" so be it.

Distance: 1.6-mile loop
Physical difficulty: Moderate
Technical difficulty: Moderate
Trail surface: Packed singletrack and slickrock
Navigation tips: The base of the loop connects to Cross Canyon (GPS: N 38 42.852' / W 109 38.743'). The upper part connects to Borderline (GPS: N 38 43.066' / W 109 38.424'). Feel free to take an extra lap.

Cross Canyon

You might never guess this, but Cross Canyon cuts across the whole area, connecting Borderline to Dunestone, Secret Passage, Snippit, and Wahoo. While useful as a connector, it's definitely a fun ride in its own right. Simply a well-built trail that is fun coming or going.

Distance: 1.3 miles point to point
Physical difficulty: Moderate
Technical difficulty: Moderate
Trail surface: Packed singletrack
Navigation tips: Cross Canyon is great way to connect the upper parking lot to Wahoo. At some point during or after riding here, remember to send good vibes to those that made these trails possible (GPS: N 38 42.276' / W 109 38.724').

Secret Passage

This short jaunt on a ribbon of red winds back and forth into and out of a secret valley. OK, so it isn't really a secret. But it is red, and the trail turns back and forth like a kids' slot-car set that came without any straight pieces. What might be a bit of a secret is that the climb out of here is pretty steep.

Distance: 0.7 mile
Physical difficulty: Moderately strenuous—but short
Technical difficulty: Moderate
Trail surface: Packed singletrack
Navigation tips: Not much to navigate. Both ends connect to Cross Canyon (GPS: N 38 42.515' / W 109 38.767').

Dunestone

Some trails have obscure names. Some are named after famous people. And some are just named for what they are. Apparently, the Klonzo Trails are the latter. Dunestone runs across the white sandstone for some slickrock fun. I can't help but think this wasn't as bumpy when it was a sand dune. Keep your eyes open to keep your Klonzo dreams pleasant ones.

Distance: 1.6-mile loop with 2 long strings attached
Physical difficulty: Moderately strenuous
Technical difficulty: Moderately challenging
Trail surface: Slickrock and singletrack. The slickrock is pocked full of bumps.

Navigation tips: Dunestone connects straight to the lower parking area, making it ideal for the final trail. If you parked in the upper lot . . . not so much. Though, the trip back on Borderline isn't too bad (GPS: N 38 42.439' / W 109 38.769').

Boondocks

The naming convention continues. Boondocks is a single-track trail that meanders out on the west side of the area. You may enjoy riding out in the boondocks so much that you take another lap here too.

Distance: 1.2-mile loop
Physical difficulty: Moderate, but getting back to Dunestone is a bit strenuous
Technical difficulty: Moderate, but getting back to Dunestone is a bit tricky

Trail surface: Packed singletrack and some slickrock
Navigation tips: Can only be reached by Dunestone (GPS: N 38 42.492' / W 109 39.047').

Snippet

A short connector.

Distance: 0.15 mile point to point
Physical difficulty: Moderate
Technical difficulty: Moderate
Trail surface: Packed singletrack and some rocks on an old road

Navigation tips: Snippet connects Borderline to Cross Canyon (GPS: N 38 42.758' / W 109 38.491').

The Ride

0.0 From the lower parking lot, head up the Borderline trail.

0.4 Upper parking lot. Continue on Borderline.

0.5 Stay right on Borderline as Cross Canyon splits off to the left.

0.9 Stay right on Borderline at this junction with Cross Canyon. You'll be here again later.

1.2 Stay on Borderline as Snippet heads up to the left.

1.7 Upon reaching Wahoo, turn right to go counterclockwise around this loop.

2.9 Unless you want to loop around Wahoo again, keep right onto Cross Canyon.

3.2 Keep right on Cross Canyon as you pass by Snippet.

3.3 Keep left at this junction with Secret Passage.

3.6 Junction with Borderline (0.9). Continue on Cross Canyon.

3.8 Continue toward the left on Cross Canyon as Secret Passage rejoins on the right.

3.9 Keep left on Cross Canyon as Dunestone departs on the right.

4.2 Turn right onto Borderline and continue past the upper parking lot to the lower parking lot.

4.7 Arrive back at the parking lot. Ready for another lap?

5 **Sovereign Singletrack**

Awesome singletrack among a bunch of multiuse trails makes for a nice day of riding. The colors are stunning as well. Speaking of colors, the slickrock on Sovereign is blazed with painted blue dashes. Good flow and fun technical challenges await you. But Sovereign is much more than that. This is a desert immersion experience. Copper Ridge Road connects Sovereign to Klondike in the north, and Klonzo is just east of the southern trailhead, allowing for many different epic journeys. The Salt Wash singletrack is another north–south trail that runs alongside Sovereign. It permits motorcycles and has some challenging technical terrain. Its slickrock portions are blazed with green paint. The connectors between the two trails are blazed in black. The Pipeline road can even be taken southward to connect this region to the Brand Trail system.

Location: 15 miles north of Moab

Distance: 9.5-mile loop

Riding time: 2 hours as described. A week's worth of variety.

Physical difficulty: Moderately strenuous

Technical difficulty: Moderately challenging with some spots you may wish to walk

Trail surface: Singletrack and slickrock in all their forms. Packed dirt, rocky, ledgy, smooth, and, yes, even a bit of sand.

Land status: BLM

Maps: USGS Merrimac Butte and Klondike Bluffs

Finding the trailhead: Drive north 12.8 miles from Center Street and Main on US 191. Turn right onto Willow Springs Road. Stay on Willow Springs Road for 2 miles to reach the trailhead on the left. At 1.6 miles down the road you'll have to cross Willow Creek, which is usually dry but

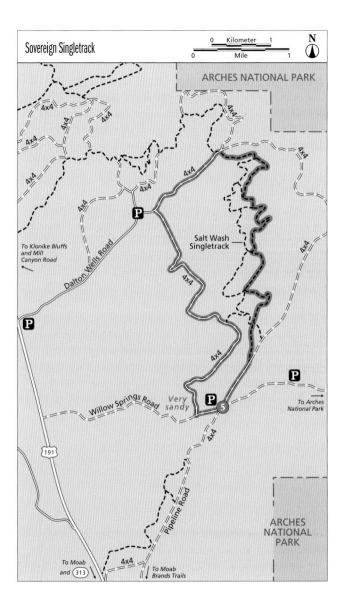

Sovereign Singletrack

ARCHES NATIONAL PARK

4x4
4x4
4x4
4x4
4x4
4x4
4x4
4x4
4x4
4x4

To Klonike Bluffs and Mill Canyon Road

Dalton Wells Road

Salt Wash Singletrack

4x4

4x4

Willow Springs Road

Very sandy

5

To Arches National Park

4x4

191

Pipeline Road

To Moab and 313

4x4

To Moab Brands Trails

ARCHES NATIONAL PARK

0   Kilometer   1

0   Mile   1

N

often very sandy. If you don't have a strong SUV, you may wish to park closer to US 191 and ride to the trailhead. If you want skip Moab and go directly to Sovereign from I-70, it's 18.5 miles to Willow Springs Road. Trailhead GPS: N38 41.880' / W109 39.911'

Alternatively, you can access things from the north via Dalton Wells Road. Drive 13.9 miles from downtown Moab or 17.4 miles from I-70. After the turn continue 1.7 miles to the parking area. You can even take the Moab Brands trail to the pipeline road and ride to the southern trailhead that way.

The Ride

0.0   From the southern trailhead's parking lot, head east (left). (Did you know Head East was a band?)

0.1   Pretty much immediately after leaving the lot, turn left and head up the Pipeline Road.

0.6   The singletrack veers away to the left off of the road. GPS: N38 42.273' / W109 39.497'.

1.0   Intersection with the Salt Wash portion of singletrack. The main Sovereign route continues straight and is marked with blue paint as it crosses slickrock. The Salt Wash trail is more technical and allows ATVs and motorcycles and thus has some pretty loose ascents. It's probably best to ride Salt Wash southbound if you choose to ride it.

1.8   Stay right as a connector to Salt Wash leaves to the left.

2.5   Keep right as another connector leads to Salt Wash.

3.5   Keep right as yet another connector heads to Salt Wash. Some *extremely* tight switchbacks lie ahead.

3.8   Keep right—you guessed it—another connector to Salt Wash.

4.4   Cross over the Salt Wash trail at this four-way intersection. Left heads down toward your vehicle while right climbs steeply up to the southern end of the slickrock playground.

5.0 Dalton Wells Road. This description turns left here and follows the road for an easier way back to the vehicle. Plenty of riders will look at the map for more options here or you may want to simply retrace the route. To get the last bit of Sovereign Singletrack from here, head into the dry wash and follow the trail out and to the right (north).

5.9 Turn left on the road that T's into this one. It's easy to see but easy to miss. If you reach a big Y intersection, you've missed it and have almost reached the Dalton Wells Road trailhead.

9.3 Ignoring any side trails, you reach Willow Springs Road. Turn left toward the trailhead.

9.5 Arrive back at the trailhead.

6 Klondike Bluffs Mountain Biking Area

Klondike Bluffs has its roots in the old Jeep trails that climbed up the white Entrada sandstone. Back in the day, this was thought of as a "beginners" trail for novice riders to get used to Moab's rough terrain. As the masses descended upon the region, Klondike Bluffs blossomed into the ever-expanding system here today, which offers something for riders of every ability and fitness level, allowing riders to tailor their routes. Awesome flowing singletrack, rugged technical tests, riding among dinosaurs, endless loops, and a nice hike into Arches National Park are all available here. What will you do-oo-oo for a ride here?

Location: 16 miles north of Moab

Distance: From 1.0 mile to as much as you'd like. The classic ride here is an 8.8-mile out and back from the southern trailhead.

Riding time: About 1 to 3 hours. If you ride the classic route, allow extra time to hike into Arches National Park for lunch.

Physical difficulty: The area's trails run the gamut from easy to strenuous.

Technical difficulty: Easy (Agate) to challenging (EKG)

Trail surface: Flowing singletrack, rocks, erosion, some sand traps and white, lumpy sandstone

Land status: State and BLM land bordering Arches National Park

Maps: USGS Klondike Bluffs; Trail Mix has posted detailed map signs at nearly every junction.

Finding the trailhead: There are two main trailheads for the Klondike Bluffs Mountain Biking Area: North and South. Both lie on dirt roads that should be passable by most vehicles. The area is interwoven with singletrack that is accessible from the north or south. The area is rich with

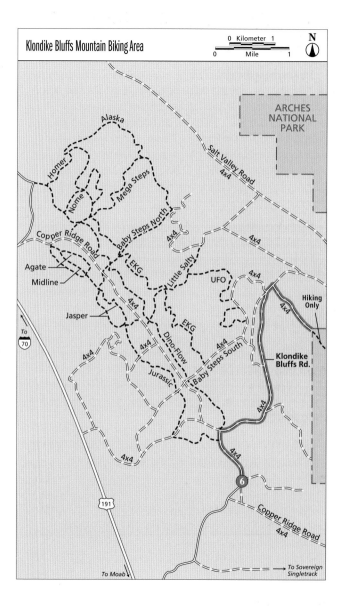

Klondike Bluffs Mountain Biking Area

0 Kilometer 1

0 Mile 1

N

ARCHES NATIONAL PARK

Alaska

Homer

Nome

Mega Steps

Baby Steps North

Salt Valley Road

4x4

4x4

4x4

Copper Ridge Road

Agate

Midline

EKG

Little Salty

UFO

4x4

4x4

Hiking Only

Jasper

4x4

EKG

Klondike Bluffs Rd.

Dino-Flow

4x4

To 70

4x4

4x4

Jurassic

Baby Steps South

4x4

4x4

4x4

6

191

Copper Ridge Road

4x4

To Moab

To Sovereign Singletrack

clay deposits, and the roads can be slippery when wet. Erosion can also carve some grooves in the road. If you must, park in the area provided on US 191 en route to the southern trailhead.

Southern trailhead: The southern trailhead lies 16.5 miles north on US 191 from Center Street in Moab, then 2.8 miles up a dirt road. After passing mile marker 142, look for the right-hand turn lane in 0.5 mile, signed for Klondike Bluffs. Follow the dirt road north. Keep left on the main road through the rolling hills 1.1 miles from the highway. At 2.6 miles keep left and continue to the trailhead, visible less than 0.2 mile ahead. GPS: N38 46.303' / W109 42.849'. There's an alternative trailhead 0.8 mile farther ahead for those with high-clearance vehicles that will power through some long sandy patches.

Northern trailhead: The northern area actually has four trailheads. To get to them, drive 22.9 miles from Center Street in Moab (6.4 miles past the turn to the southern trailhead). Turn right and drive 1.1 miles up an often-washboardy road. This is a good place for many passenger vehicles to park. GPS: N38 49.112' / W109 46.051'. Passenger vehicles can usually turn left here and continue 1 mile to the Copper Ridge Sauropod Tracksite's parking area. The road is usually well maintained for low-clearance vehicles. If you have a more rugged vehicle and are up for it, two more parking areas lie 0.5 and 0.7 mile down the right-hand fork, which is Copper Ridge Road.

....

Baby Steps

Want to get a lot of variety in one ride? Check this baby out! Sandstone? Check! Cairn-marked route finding? Check! Dinosaur tracks? Check! But don't check out. Baby Steps demands your attention. It's not a trail to zone out into a groove. It keeps your brain engaged thinking about the next test. Don't miss the well-marked turns by going too fast. Mining ruins on the upper portion conjure up Moab's other rocky past.

Distance: 15.0 miles if done as a loop
Physical difficulty: Strenuous
Technical difficulty: Challenging
Trail surface: Slickrock, singletrack, and a bit of four-wheel-drive road. Some soft patches can grab errant tires.

Navigation tips: Use Baby Steps South as an alternate for getting to Klondike Bluffs trail. Please don't ride around trail features. If it looks more like a hazard to you, please hop off and walk over it. The slickrock portions are marked with blue dashes painted on the rock (GPS: N 38 47.742' / W 109 42.377').

EKG

If you like testing your bike skills crossing up and down big slickrock cracks while gaining over 1,000 feet in altitude, then doing the same thing while losing about 1,000 feet, then EKG is your heaven. It obviously gets its name from its elevation profile, but it'll get your heart rockin'. It really is a fun trail, but less-experienced riders may want to find a way off it. Luckily, they'll have several opportunities to arrest their worries. If you have a heart monitor, hook it up and give it a workout. Don't forget to look around. This is Moab riding at its best. EKG is the real deal.

Distance: 5.3 miles point to point
Physical difficulty: Strenuous
Technical difficulty: Challenging
Trail surface: Slickrock

Navigation tips: There are a number of places to transfer to Dino-Flow. EKG is marked with orange dashes (GPS: N 38 47.116' / W 109 42.982').

UFO

This trail offers a good way to cut some sand out of a Baby Steps loop. Some tight switchbacks keep things exciting, and the packed, red-dirt singletrack gives you the feeling you're riding on Mars. Sauceresque rocks just add to the effect and may have you ducking.

Distance: 1.6 miles point to point
Physical difficulty: Moderately strenuous. You won't believe me if I tell you the change in elevation from start to finish is only 100 feet. Maybe it's that one *steep* climb.
Technical difficulty: Moderately challenging. Are there aliens in those cracks grabbing at your wheels?
Trail surface: Packed, red dirt, and slickrock. An alien probe may be making my memory a bit fuzzy, but I remember more slickrock on the north end of the trail.
Navigation tips: I think the painted dash color was chartreuse? It's a light purplish color. UFO connects Baby Steps to Little Salty. EKG to Baby Steps to UFO to Little Salty to Dino-Flow and home might be just what you're looking for (GPS: N 38 48.501' / W 109 42.903').

Little Salty

A fun way to make a loop with UFO and Baby Steps. Descend and find options with EKG, Dino-Flow, or Copper Ridge Road (Baby Steps) down in the valley. It's also a useful way up from the south to head north—to Alaska.

Distance: 1.7 miles point to point
Physical difficulty: Moderately strenuous up, moderately easy down
Technical difficulty: Moderately challenging
Trail surface: Slickrock with a bit of dirt on either end
Navigation tips: Little Salty sports lovely yellow paint dashes. The eroded upper portion can be a challenge after a heavy storm (GPS: N 38 48.248' / W 109 44.147').

Mega Steps

Mega Steps is a stairway to the heavenly view at the top of this area's northern section and serves as a main northern access point. Mega Steps is also a good downhill. It's not too steep, so it's fun either way. It seeks out slickrock, making good use of the terrain.

Distance: 3.1 miles point to point
Physical difficulty: Moderately strenuous going up
Technical difficulty: Moderately challenging
Trail surface: Slickrock, packed dirt, and broken rocks
Navigation tips: Green with envy? Sorry, bad pun. But, green

is the blaze color for Mega Steps. Mega Steps closes the loop with Alaska, connects with Baby Steps up top and EKG, Dino-Flow, and Copper Ridge Road below. There's also a trailhead at the bottom (GPS: N 38 49.181' / W 109 45.412').

Alaska

Alaska is a remote section that's worth including if you have the time and energy. It has varied terrain and expansive views and requires a fair amount of aerobic effort. Climbing Mega Steps is the easier way up. Enjoy being dwarfed by your surroundings. Alaska is big country.

Distance: 3.6 miles point to point
Physical difficulty: Strenuous
Technical difficulty: Moderately challenging
Trail surface: Slickrock and singletrack
Navigation tips: A segment here has exposure on both sides. Don't worry, just keep following

the dashes on the rock. You can tell an area has a lot of trails when one of them is blazed with teal-colored paint. Yes, teal. Oh yeah, navigation. Park at the Copper Ridge Sauropod Site and take Dino-Flow to Homer, Nome, or Mega Steps and head up (GPS: N 38 49.420' / W 109 45.040').

Nome

While in Alaska, it might be nice to visit Nome. Your dogs may get tired from the detour, but it's a fun, technical trail.

Distance: 1.9 miles point to point
Physical difficulty: Moderately strenuous
Technical difficulty: Challenging

Trail surface: Slickrock and singletrack
Navigation tips: Make a quick loop by heading down Dino-Flow,

up Mega Steps, and on to Nome. Then follow Nome back to Dino-Flow. Repeat, and don't get dizzy (GPS: N 38 49.579' / W 109 45.016').

Homer

This is the northernmost way up and the most direct route to Alaska from the northernmost trailhead. It also serves as a quick, technical descent to the Copper Ridge Sauropod parking area, which is a good place for a family with a wide range of abilities to start their day. The most accomplished can head up Homer, the middle group can roll down Dino-Flow, and the non-biker can drive the shuttle to the lower parking area. By the way, the upper parking area also has a pit toilet.

Distance: 0.7 mile point to point
Physical difficulty: Strenuous
Technical difficulty: Challenging
Trail surface: Slickrock, singletrack, and broken rocks
Navigation tips: You actually have to take a small bit of Dino-Flow to hit the trail proper. Doh! While Homer is named after a city in Alaska, the trail is blazed with Simpson-yellow paint dashes (GPS: N 38 49.771' / W 109 45.715').

Dino-Flow

A great way to descend to the lower trails to start your day or to return to the lower lot to end it. Hop on, look ahead, and flow on down the trail. A good challenge for newer riders would be to ride Dino-Flow down from Mega Steps. Park at the lower lot, ride up Jurassic and Jasper to Baby Steps North. Pick up Dino-Flow there and pour yourself back down the trail. It's the nice cousin to EKG. Riders of any level can get into a Zen-like trance flowing down among the rocks.

Distance: 5.6 miles point to point
Physical difficulty: Moderately easy
Technical difficulty: Moderately easy
Trail surface: Singletrack and slickrock
Navigation tips: The trail now starts up at the Copper Ridge Sauropod parking area. In fact, if you park by the sign, you probably stepped on it while walking around your car. It heads south past the pit toilet. When the trail is on slickrock, it's blazed with pink (GPS: N 38 49.798' / W 109 45.788').

Agate, Midline, and Jasper

The plan was for these trails to offer beginners a place to get used to riding trails, and they deliver on that promise. However, don't expect clear sailing; there is some sand. Sand is one of the tougher things for a beginner to figure out. Remember to just give the bike its head and let it float. Young riders will be enthralled with the chunks of rock lying about that give the trail its name. Each trail has a spot or two that might be best for beginners to walk. That's just fine. It'll all work out.

Distance: Agate 1.8-mile loop, Midline 0.8 mile, Jasper 1.7-mile loop
Physical difficulty: Easy
Technical difficulty: Easy with a moderately easy spot or two
Trail surface: Singletrack interspersed with chunks of agate and some pesky sand
Navigation tips: Jasper is a bit tougher than Agate. The Midline is the easiest of them all, according to adults that can ride. But beginners may have different opinions (GPS: N 38 49.088' / W 109 45.625').

Jurassic

This trail gets a beginner rating, but it seems like beginners would say it's a step harder than Agate or Jasper. The lack of sand, however, makes it seem easier to me. It feels more like a *real* trail and thus is probably more fun for an older beginner. I'm not saying that it isn't fun for more-advanced riders though. I think it's a better way to return north than Copper Ridge Road. The only drawback for a parent introducing their kids to trails would be the distance. A cutoff at Baby Steps solves that problem for most riders.

Distance: 3.0 miles point to point
Physical difficulty: Moderately easy
Technical difficulty: Moderately easy
Trail surface: Singletrack
Navigation tips: Starts at Copper Ridge Road on the left and ends at Jasper with a cutoff point at Baby Steps. Can be ridden as an even easier downhill than Dino-Flow, for beginners especially, if one parent rides with them while another drives the car from north to south and picks everyone up (GPS: N 38 46.943' / W 109 43.074').

Klondike Bluffs (Classic Route)

The classic ride here is a good first ride that offers slickrock for moderately experienced riders. The classic Klondike Bluffs helps to shed light on your slickrock skills (possessed or needed) and provides access to dinosaur tracks and expansive views. This trail accesses a variety of singletrack, allowing riders to tailor their ride. It offers dinosaur tracks, white slickrock, and a hike into Arches National Park to see the bulbous tops of Klondike Bluffs that makes a good lunch site.

Distance: 8.2 miles out and back
Technical difficulty: Moderately easy. The four-wheel-drive road and slickrock portion are moderately difficult and are typically harder going down than up for most riders.
Physical difficulty: Moderate with a couple of extended climbs. The slickrock has some steeps, but the rest is pretty gradual.
Trail surface: 5.6 miles of four-wheel-drive road and 3.2 miles on slickrock. The road tickles the tires with rocks, erosion, and some sand. The white slickrock is a bit lumpy.

The Ride

0.0 From the southern trailhead, pass through the gate and onto the road, which is now a four-wheel-drive track. High-clearance vehicles that will go through deep sand can continue farther to an alternate trailhead.

0.3 Sand trap! This is the first of two prominent sand traps. It's rideable, but getting off and pushing saves energy and equipment.

0.7 Sand trap number two.

0.8 The road forks; turn right. This should be well blazed.

1.0 A spur goes left; stay right. Look for painted dinosaur-track trail blazes on the rock. The cairns tend to be easier to spot, however.

1.2 The road becomes rocky and eroded. Thread the rocks with your knobbies.

1.6 Begin the slickrock ascent. It is strenuous going for a bit.

1.7 Bear left, staying on the edge of the rock.

1.8 Start looking for real dinosaur tracks. The big ones are about 1 foot long and may be circled with rocks. A particularly nice set is preserved at the slickrock's edge as the route bears up to the right. They've been described as birdlike. Definitely not your average roadrunner!

2.1 Crank through a brief dirt section bearing left, then up the slickrock bearing right.

2.2 Be careful crossing the moderate-to-challenging dip on the slickrock to the right, then keep following cairns.

2.3 A huge cairn sits atop this viewpoint. The trail turns left and down briefly before turning right and up the slickrock. Missing the turn leads down the four-wheel-drive road and skips a wonderful section of slickrock.

3.3 Ignore the faint road that heads down the wash on the right. Stay on the main road. Note this spot to avoid a wrong turn on the way back.

3.5 The road forks; go right. Left leads over to Salt Valley.

3.8 Keep left. Right fizzles into a crypto-crust abuse situation.

4.1 Stay left to finish the ride by climbing technical singletrack. Right is a short trip to an abandoned mining site.

4.4 End of the line. Park your bike and hike up to see into Arches National Park. Stay right and walk up onto the slickrock. Cairns lead the way to a fabulous view of the Klondike Cliffs. Retrace the route home.

8.8 Arrive back at the trailhead.

7 **Hidden Canyon**

Only nature could craft something so perfectly chaotic. Parallel rings of color, barely tilted, rise above the sand and brush floor. Each seemingly insignificant groove helps continue the sculpting of this treasure. Leading to the canyon, blankets of wrinkled white sandstone provide three expansive play areas, the third bordered by a wire-thin canyon. The actual Hidden Canyon bursts suddenly upon riders who pedal onward after crossing the wire canyon's head on a sandy road. This area has seen a lot of abuse. Please read the section on cryptobiotic crust under "Riding Right!" in the introduction before setting out on this ride.

Location: 20 miles north of Moab

Distance: 7.4 miles out and back minimum. Plenty of play areas can add distance.

Riding time: About 1 to 2 hours allows only minimal play time

Physical difficulty: Moderate. Many novices will find this aerobically acceptable.

Technical difficulty: Moderate to challenging. The roads to the play areas are moderate, while the slickrock can be challenging, depending upon the chosen path.

Trail surface: 6.8 miles on four-wheel-drive road; it's up to you on the slickrock. The four-wheel-drive road is initially eroded dirt. The latter parts of the ride are very sandy. The slickrock offers expansive playgrounds of white sandstone. The access road becomes gooey when wet and should be avoided after a storm.

Land status: BLM

Map: USGS Jug Rock

Finding the trailhead: From Moab drive 17.1 miles north on US 191 to Blue Hills Road and turn left (GPS N38 44.906' / W109 44.292'). Take the right fork at mile 19.4 (2.3 miles from US 191). Continue and

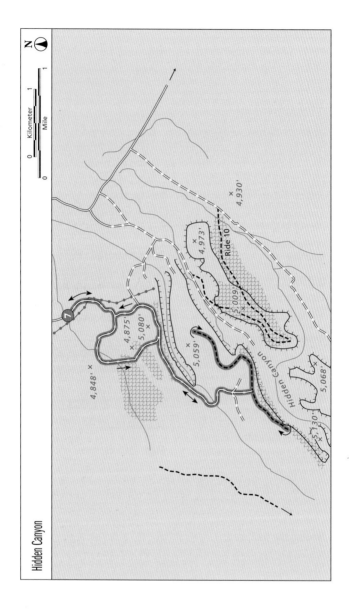

Hidden Canyon

turn left at mile 20.7 (3.6) onto a dirt spur (GPS: N38 44.664' / W109 46.786'). Stay left at mile 21 (3.9) where another road joins. After crossing a wash at mile 21.4 (4.3), look for a parking area on the right. GPS: N38 44.081' / W109 48.040'

The Ride

0.0   Pedal south on the road.

0.3   Keep right and pass through a fence. This is an alternate parking spot and the beginning of the ride's longest climb.

0.6   Stay right. The road to the left is the return route.

0.8   Stay left through this zone. The road is packed dirt with rocks and some sand.

1.1   Keep left here.

1.2   Enter the first slickrock playground. It's the right, or northernmost, slickrock of the two formations that have been visible. When playing here avoid areas of soil! Please stay off the cryptobiotic crust.

1.4   The exit from this play area is 0.2 mile from the entrance on the left edge of the rock. A cairn marks the crossover point to the next playground. It's best to find this spot before exploring the slickrock too far. Return here when ready to cross over and stop on the ridge. From here you can see how to exit across the rock. It's about 0.2 mile straight across to the steep, eroded road that continues the ride. (Remember: These odometer readings don't count exploratory miles.)

1.7   After the second playground, the exit crosses over a low ridge and into another slickrock zone joining another four-wheel-drive road. The road runs west and south for 1.4 miles, then crosses over a wash (at mile 3.1) and heads to the payoff of the ride. Advanced riders will enjoy some fabulous terrain left of this road while heading for the crossover point. Play "keep off the crust" and have fun.

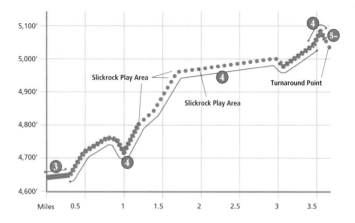

3.1 This is the crossover point. Turn left onto the sandy doubletrack.

3.5 Stay straight at this three-way intersection.

3.7 Wow! Gawk at Hidden Canyon. Wipe your chin before heading out onto this exposed rock. Use good crust ethics and mind the edges. Don't try to get to the bottom—the only route involves rock climbing. Besides, the bottom is too sandy to be enjoyable. Retrace the route back to the crossover at mile 1.7. Then stay right and continue down the road. Roll another 1.1 miles to the trailhead.

7.4 Arrive back at the parking area.

8 Tusher Canyon's Left Side

Looking for limitless slickrock fun? This is my favorite place to play! It takes some effort and attention to get on top of this rock, but once you do they may never get you to come down. Pack a lunch (and maybe the headphones with a tape of Ennio Morricone's "Fistful of Dollars") and create slickrock splendor. There's about a mile of sand to endure before reaching the canyon's rock, but this is avoidable with a four-wheeler.

Location: 17 miles north of Moab

Distance: 8.8 miles out and back minimum from 2-wheel-drive trailhead. If you have a sturdy vehicle and are comfortable with some sand, follow the ride description to shave off the 2.5-mile dirt road ride and park at the alternate trailhead.

Riding time: About 2 hours plus play time

Physical difficulty: Moderate. The sand saps even the strongest legs, so count on walking. The initial slickrock climb is on the steep side. But once on top, the terrain mellows out.

Technical difficulty: Moderate to challenging. The sand, if ridden, is a technical hassle. But the slickrock is awesome! It can be made technically easier or harder depending on your visual acuity and your route choice. In short, the line you choose should be your own.

Trail surface: The ride to the slickrock is on a dirt road that is very sandy for the last mile. The slickrock is expansive, sticky, orange, and pretty—some of the region's best.

Land status: BLM

Map: USGS Jug Rock

Finding the trailhead: From Center Street in Moab, drive 15.4 miles north on US 191. Turn left onto Mill Canyon Road (GPS: N38 43.628' / W109 43.341'), go 0.6 mile from US 191, and park in the lot on the right (GPS: N38 43.530' / W109 43.950'). If you have a sturdy vehicle and are comfortable with some sand, follow the ride description to shave off

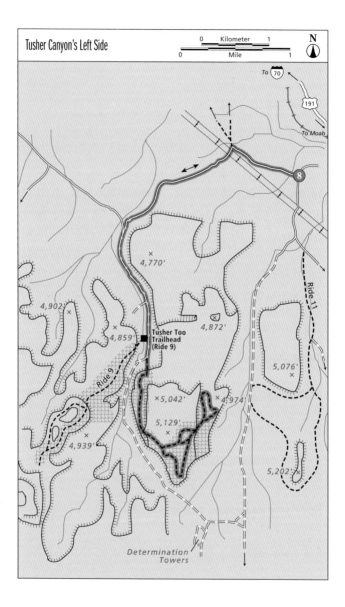

0   Kilometer   1

0   Mile   1

N

To 70

191

To Moab

8

×
4,770'

Ride 11

4,902'
×

×
4,859'

Tusher Too
Trailhead
(Ride 9)

×
4,872'

×
5,076'

Ride 9

×5,042'   ×4,974'

5,129'
×

×
4,939'

5,202'
×

Determination
Towers

the 2.5-mile dirt road ride and park at the alternate trailhead (GPS: N38 42.798' / W109 45.658').

The Ride

0.0 Take the road out the back of the parking lot to the northwest.

0.1 Stay right at this fork.

0.6 The road goes under the power lines.

2.0 The road makes a hard right but this route follows the wash to the left.

2.5 This is a good place to park if conditions are good. It's typically too sandy to ride well. Hope for damp, firm tread to begin here. GPS: N38 42.798' / W109 45.658'

2.7 A spur heads up to the right. Remain in the wash.

3.4 Ride up the long, obscure, eroded rock "ramp" that leaves the wash on the left at about a 30-degree angle. This grooved rock road heads up to the slickrock formation away from the demon sand!

3.5 Look for a way up to the left of the rock knob, or plan on portaging up a rockslide. The gray rock below the slide rims out.

3.6 Weave through the rockslide. Dismount for the final 30 yards and lift your bike up the rock ledge. Cairns should help guide the way.

3.7 A geologic marker ensures you are on track after hopping up the ledge.

4.0 Look for a way up two rings of rock and continue to advance, keeping as far left as possible as the route gets skinny.

4.3 Portage up one more layer as the trail gets pinched around the corner.

4.4 Another geological marker marks a good place to start looking for a route to the right of Tusher's Tiny Tower. If you pass on the left via

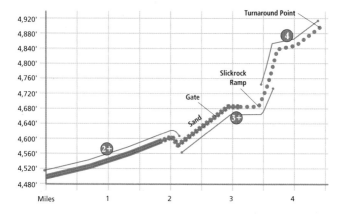

the white rock, you'll need to hunt for an environmentally friendly way back to the red rock. Route finding is now up to your own cerebellum. Before rushing off, look around and pick out something to use as a return landmark. Free-form fun awaits. Wander about a mile to the left to find a prehistoric half-pipe. But don't dive into its potholes or off the cliff at the end! When you're done, retrace the route home.

8.8 Arrive back at the parking lot.

9 Tusher Too—Tusher Canyon's Right Side

Not as expansive as Tusher's Left Side, this ride puts the same smooth stone beneath the rubber, and its access is easier. Some exploration at the terminus of the ride is nice. But please don't do any more damage than has already occurred. If you can't find the crossover at mile 5.8, go back.

Location: 15 miles north of Moab

Distance: 8.8 miles out and back. A four-wheel-drive vehicle can get you farther in, reducing the ride to 4 miles.

Riding time: About 2 to 3 hours

Physical difficulty: Moderate

Technical difficulty: Moderate to challenging. The slickrock offers both easier and harder lines—moderate to challenging is the average. The sand definitely adds to the initial difficulty.

Trail surface: The ride in is on a dirt road. The fun part is on slickrock that provides endless exploration.

Land status: BLM

Map: USGS Jug Rock

Finding the trailhead: From Center Street in Moab, drive 15.4 miles north on US 191. Turn left onto Mill Canyon Road (GPS: N38 43.628' / W109 43.341') and go 0.6 mile from US 191 and park in the lot on the right (GPS: N38 43.530' / W109 43.950'). If you have a sturdy vehicle and are comfortable with some sand, follow the ride description to shave off the dirt road ride and park at the alternate trailhead (GPS: N38 42.798' / W109 45.658').

The Ride

0.0 Follow the directions from Tusher Canyon's Left Side (Ride 8). Pick up this description at the alternate trailhead at mile 2.5.

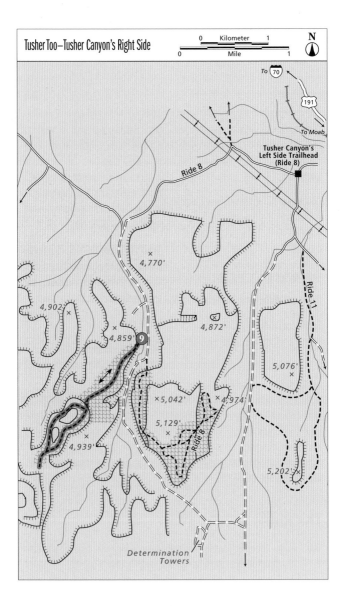

0   Kilometer   1

0   Mile   1

N

To 70

191

To Moab

**Tusher Canyon's
Left Side Trailhead
(Ride 8)**

Ride 8

Ride 11

× 4,770'

× 4,872'

× 4,902'

× 4,859'

9

× 5,076'

× 5,042'

× 4,974'

5,129' ×

Ride 8

5,202' ×

4,939' ×

*Determination
Towers*

2.5 This is a good place to park if conditions are good. It's typically too sandy to ride well. Hope for damp, firm tread to begin here. GPS: N38 42.798' / W109 45.658'.

2.6 The wash widens and the road stays to the left side. Look for another wash to enter from the right. A small sandy trail takes off from here up to the rock formation that is Tusher's Right Side.

2.8 Stay on the sandy trail as it passes beneath a rockslide. Once on the rock, pick a line and go. A good rule of thumb is to keep the overhanging layer close at hand on the right.

3.3 A glance to the left reveals the Determination Towers through the gap off the end of Tusher's Left Side.

3.8 Time to turn right and head uphill; the lower layer is history. Lift over the 4-foot ledge, then ride straight up the rock if you can.

3.9 Turn left and follow the route as it contours around the rock. Close examination reveals a trail coming over from the other side of the ridge. This is the trail mentioned at mile 4.4 for those exploring further.

4.3 The route once again pinches out. Head uphill to the top of the saddle.

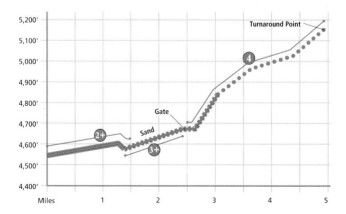

4.4 The top of the saddle. From here you can turn around and retrace your tracks down the rock, pick a fresh line, or continue to the right around the other side of the ridge. Continuing around adds some portaging and requires extreme care to keep from damaging the environment. It's not recommended. If you do go, the crossover point is at mile 5.8 or so by a tiny wash that spills into the rock. A small cairn may mark the trail. If you can't find the route, return. Please don't make a new trail!

8.8 Arrive back at the trailhead.

10 **Bartlett Wash**

Rock and roll! For those who aren't compelled to stay within the lines, this may be the best slickrock riding around. The orange rock offers bowls and climbs as well as breathtaking cliff sides. Photographers, bring your cameras! Magazine-quality photos are found here—orange rock with a deep-blue sky background. Voilà! There are eight walk-in campsites at the trailhead nestled beneath a stately old cottonwood tree. The Jedi Slickrock, also accessed here, is the southern hunk of rock. Bartlett is the northern hunk.

Location: 18 miles north of Moab

Distance: 6.2-mile loop or 4.0 miles out and back

Riding time: About 1 hour minimum. Plan on a lot of play time on Bartlett's playground!

Physical difficulty: Moderate. Gradual lines up the rock are easy to find.

Technical difficulty: Moderate to challenging. How technical do you want it? The free-form nature of the ride allows route selection from moderate to challenging.

Trail surface: 2.9 miles on slickrock; 3.3 miles on four-wheel-drive road. This is primo rock candy! When ridden as a loop, count on some extremely sandy four-wheel-drive road. The amount of bikeable slickrock is limited only by the imagination and cliffs. The access road becomes gooey when wet, making access a four-wheel-drive affair.

Land status: BLM

Map: USGS Jug Rock

Finding the trailhead: From Center Street in Moab, drive 15.4 miles north on US 191. Turn left onto Mill Canyon Road (GPS: N38 43.628' / W109 43.341'), go 0.6 mile from US 191, and turn into the lot on the right. Drive through the lot and exit via the road on the northwest corner. Continue 2.9 miles on the main road. Turn left onto Bartlett Wash Road, then keep right at the next 2 forks. Drive 0.9 mile to the trailhead. If you're not comfortable

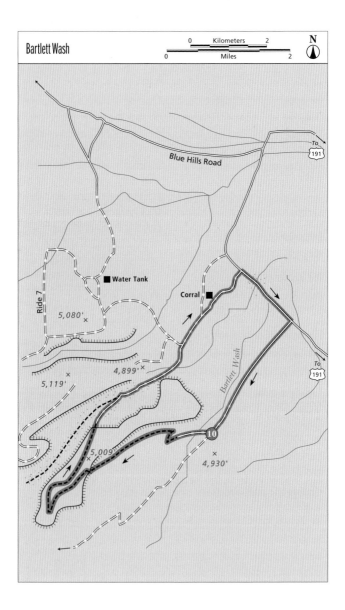

Bartlett Wash

bringing your vehicle down this road, park in the lot 0.6 mile from US 191 (GPS: N38 43.530' / W109 43.950'). You can also take Blue Hills Road to the trailhead. Drive 17.1 miles north on US 191. Turn left onto Blue Hills Road (GPS N38 44.906' / W109 44.292') and go 2.3 miles, then turn left onto another dirt road (N38 44.674' / W109 46.791'). Drive 0.8 mile to a fork in the road. Go left. (The right fork leads up to the alternate parking for those following the loop option.) Drive 0.9 mile to the trailhead, keeping right at two spurs along the way. GPS: N38 43.046' / W109 47.119'

The Ride

0.0 From the parking area follow the road to the left, away from US 191.

0.1 Follow the trail on the right to the slickrock. Climb up onto the rock, and head up and left. Stay on the flat rock, continuing to head left. To access Jedi Slickrock, continue 0.1 mile. The trailhead will be on the left.

0.4 Hop up the ledge's low point and switchback to gain some elevation. Then quickly turn back to the left and continue following the rock strata.

0.7 Cross the sand to the next rock section.

0.8 At the next rock stay low on the lighter-colored layer. It's free-form from here.

2.1 If you went straight for the tip of the rock, this mileage is close. It continues to be rideable around this point to the other side of the canyon. I recommend playing around, then finding a route back the way you came to get maximum slickrock pleasure. But for those who must ride in loops, the description continues. But really . . . go back the way you came.

2.8 A couple of hairy, exposed sidehills are necessary to clean the descent to the valley. Portage your bike, carefully.

3.0 Drop onto the valley floor at this insanely sandy road. It weaves in and out of the wash without any real relief from the sand.

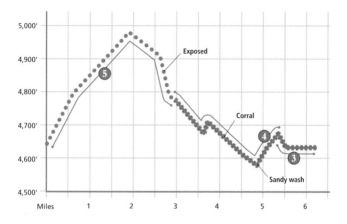

3.9 Finally the sand gives way to a packed-sediment descent and rocky climb. The going is much better from now on.

4.3 Stay right past the spurs, arriving at a corral. Turn right here, and descend to the main access road. Left heads to the same road but farther from the car. This corral makes a good alternate trailhead.

4.7 Turn right at this T intersection and find the car. This is the road in the access directions. Follow it across the wash and up the hill.

5.3 Turn right on this road.

6.2 Complete the loop. Keep in mind that mileages are without any slickrock playing. Yours will probably be higher.

11 **Monitor and Merrimac**

Monitor and Merrimac Buttes are named after the old Civil War ironside ships. Here they fight in a sea of sand. History buffs will recognize their shapes instantly as the Monitor on the left and the Merrimac on the right. Both buttes offer slickrock playgrounds, but it takes riding past the Abominable Sand Monster to get there. The current rendition of this trail is much more rideable and has plenty of slickrock as well. The day after a rain is the time to try heading all the way to the buttes. The current trail is shorter, eliminating the sandfest journey to the Monitor and Merrimac. It looks like the Abominable Sand Monster has won this battle. But perhaps we've won the war. The new rendition has plenty of tasty slickrock without the pain of pushing a bike through a sea of sand. It's probably time you gave this trail a quick look.

Location: 16 miles north of Moab off US 191

Distance: 4.5-mile balloon loop

Riding time: About 1 hour plus slickrock play time

Physical difficulty: Moderate

Technical difficulty: Moderate. The slickrock can serve up challenging delights.

Trail surface: Singletrack, slickrock, and dirt road

Land status: BLM

Maps: USGS Merrimac Butte, Jug Rock

Finding the trailhead: From Center Street in Moab, drive 15.4 miles north on US 191. Turn left onto Mill Canyon Road (GPS: N38 43.628' / W109 43.341'), go 0.6 mile from US 191, and pass by a lot on the right (GPS: N38 43.530' / W109 43.950'). Continue 0.4 mile and turn right into the parking area. There is also parking available 0.8 mile farther ahead by turning right in 0.1 mile and continuing to the Mill Canyon Dinosaur Trail. GPS: N 38 42.741 ' / W 109 44.374 '

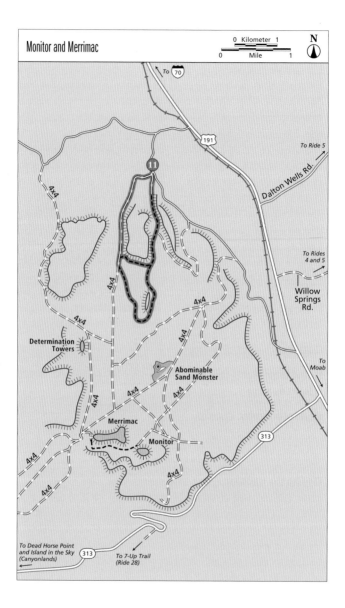

Monitor and Merrimac

0 Kilometer 1
0 Mile 1

N

To 70

191

To Ride 5

Dalton Wells Rd.

11

To Rides 4 and 5

Willow Springs Rd.

To Moab

4x4

Determination Towers

Abominable Sand Monster

4x4

4x4

Merrimac

Monitor

313

4x4

To Dead Horse Point and Island in the Sky (Canyonlands)

313

To 7-Up Trail (Ride 28)

The Ride

0.0   From the parking area turn right (south) and start down the road.

0.1   Keep straight. The road to the left goes to the Mill Canyon Dinosaur Trail, which also serves as an alternate trailhead for this route.

0.2   Bear right here as the main road bears left.

0.6   Keep right again. Left goes around the butte to your left and can loop back to the fork at mile 0.2, but the Abominable Sand Monster is out there—somewhere—lurking.

0.8   This is where the balloon loop starts. When you get back here, you'll retrace the route back to the trailhead. Follow the singletrack onto the slickrock.

2.8   The trail has looped all the way around the rock outcropping and now dances with the road to the Mill Canyon Dinosaur Trail. If you want to see that, it's 0.9 mile north to its parking area. Otherwise, look for this trail's signage to point you back onto the slickrock to complete the balloon loop.

3.0   The singletrack leaves the road to the right (east) and returns to slickrock.

3.7   Back at the 0.8-mile spot and time to retrace the route to the trailhead.

4.5   Arrive back at the trailhead.

12 **Top of the World**

Sing along with Karen Carpenter: "I'm on the . . . top of the world, looking . . . down on creation and the only explanation I can find" is that, as tough as this trail is physically, its beauty is worth the trip. The Mystery and Titan Towers jut up from below; the La Sals rise to the south; and the rock formations—Coffee Pot, Covenant, Mother Superior, Priest and Nuns, and the tip of Castle Rock—are all visible. On a clear day you can see into Colorado and the highlands to the north. Parriott Mesa and Arches National Park are also in sight.

Location: 33 miles northeast of Moab

Distance: 18.8 miles out and back; 8.6 miles if riding from the alternate trailhead

Riding time: About 3 hours; 1.5 hours from the alternate trailhead

Physical difficulty: Strenuous. The climb alone is steep. Pair that with the technical nature of the trail, and the result is rubber legs and aching lungs.

Technical difficulty: Moderate to challenging. The obstacles are frequent and occur on steeps requiring good rubber-legged, rock-hopping abilities.

Trail surface: 10.3 miles on gravel road; 8.5 miles on four-wheel-drive road. The four-wheel-drive road consists of broken slickrock, packed dirt, and slickrock proper.

Land status: BLM

Maps: USGS Dewey, Blue Chief Mesa, Fisher Towers

Finding the trailhead: From Center and Main Streets in Moab, drive 2.6 miles north on US 191. Turn right onto UT 128. Pass by Matrimony Springs (see the "Water" section in the introduction). About 33.6 miles from Center Street, turn right onto a dirt road that leaves the highway in the middle of a curve. It's tough to see—the gap in the guardrail is slim. (If you miss it, you'll immediately run onto the modern version

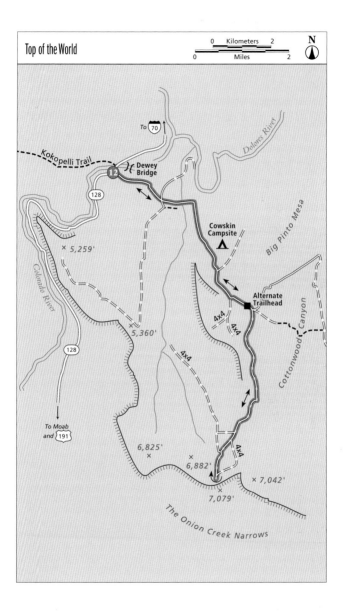

Kilometers

Miles

N

To 70

Dolores River

Kokopelli Trail

12

Dewey Bridge

128

Cowskin Campsite

Big Pinto Mesa

× 5,259'

Colorado River

× 5,360'

4x4

4x4

Alternate Trailhead

Cottonwood Canyon

128

4x4

To Moab and 191

6,825' ×

× 6,882'

4x4

× 7,042'

× 7,079'

The Onion Creek Narrows

of Dewey Bridge spanning the Colorado River.) Pass the parking area provided next to the old Dewey Bridge and drive about 200 yards to a dirt parking area. GPS: N38 48.635' / W109 17.908'. If that's full, there is one more parking area another 100 yards up the road. If the road has recently been graded, however, a family car can make it farther down the washboarded road an additional 5 miles to the alternate trailhead. GPS: N38 46.236' / W109 14.989'. The alternate trailhead cuts 10 miles out of this loop, giving you more energy to tackle the brutal climb that is Top of the World. If you don't want such a long trail, try the Pole Canyon Rim option.

The Ride

0.0 Head southeast up the gravel road, away from Dewey Bridge. Avoid all spurs for 5.1 miles. The road rolls up and down before settling into a constant climb.

1.1 Intersection. Stay on the main road. The road to the right heads up to the Pole Canyon Rim.

3.4 The road passes a couple of slickrock playgrounds, then Cowskin Campsite comes up on the left. The road turns right and grows steeper.

4.5 A spur goes right. No matter how much you wish for this to be the route, it's not. Keep on the main road.

5.0 A back-road junction marks the alternate trailhead. The gravel road bends left and then goes downhill. Instead, turn right onto the four-wheel-drive road and keep right. The four-wheel-drive road going left heads to Dolores River Overlook. Stay right for this ride and the Kokopelli Trail (see appendix A: Kokopelli Trail).

5.1 A well-signed junction points right to Top of the World. Left is the Kokopelli Trail.

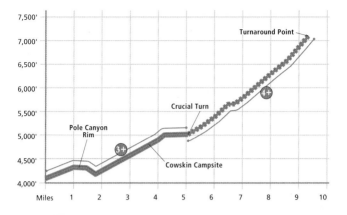

5.3 Leave the gate as is.

5.4 Begin a 0.3-mile slickrock ascent.

5.8 Stay left as a spur heads right. Yup, keep climbing. Looking down makes it seem less steep.

6.8 Bear right as a faint old road continues ahead.

7.1 Surprise! The climb eases for a rare break.

7.4 Back into the climb and it's getting more technical.

8.1 Stay left on the slickrock as a faint road leaves to the right.

8.4 At a fork in the road marked with a cairn, veer right and up broken slickrock. This is the final stretch.

9.4 Stop! The slickrock ahead goes straight to the cliff's edge, then drops about 2,400 feet. After the long climb the stupendous vistas are a welcome excuse to take a rest. When your soul is full, turn around and follow your tire tracks for the white-knuckle descent to the trailhead.

18.8 Arrive back at the trailhead.

Option: Turning right at the 1.1-mile mark leads to Pole Canyon Rim. You're the king of the world at this vantage point, looking down on the Colorado River and the boaters going by. But be careful—watching the power lines descend into the valley induces vertigo. The best biking part of this trip is the downhill, which is uncrowded and fast. The climb is shorter and easier than Top of the World, but the view, while spectacular, isn't as far-reaching.

13 **Onion Creek**

Riding in a twisted landscape of deep reds and strange whites is otherworldly. No wonder movies are shot in this area so often. Picture John Wayne riding his steed down, down, and farther down from the mesa tops to the bottoms in Professor Valley. One major uphill slaps riders in the face at mile 14.3. The only real problem with the ride is the extreme shuttle, but it's worth it! Bring a towel and a dry set of clothes to keep the inside of your cars clean. *Caution:* Don't ride this if there is a chance of flooding. Getting caught in the narrows in a flood will carry you downstream in a manner that the human body was not designed for.

Location: 35 miles east of Moab

Distance: 26.2 miles point to point

Riding time: About 3 hours (plus a long shuttle)

Physical difficulty: Moderate. A great deal of the workout will be upper body. There is one nasty hill that begins at mile 14.3.

Technical difficulty: Moderate. Speed, creek crossings, and erosion will make your eyes water. Or is it the onions?

Trail surface: 26.2 miles on four-wheel-drive road. When wet the route is slick and best avoided. The route crosses Onion Creek countless times, making for a wet and wild ride. It's no use trying to keep dry.

Land status: Manti-La Sal National Forest, BLM, and private holdings

Maps: USGS Mount Waas, Fisher Valley, Fisher Towers

Finding the trailhead: First drop off a shuttle vehicle at the ride's end. From Moab drive 2.6 miles north on US 191 to UT 128. Turn right and drive 22 miles northeast to Onion Creek Road (passing Castleton Road on the right 16.1 miles from US 191—the road to the trailhead). Park the shuttle car at the endpoint trailhead's parking area 0.7 mile down Onion Creek

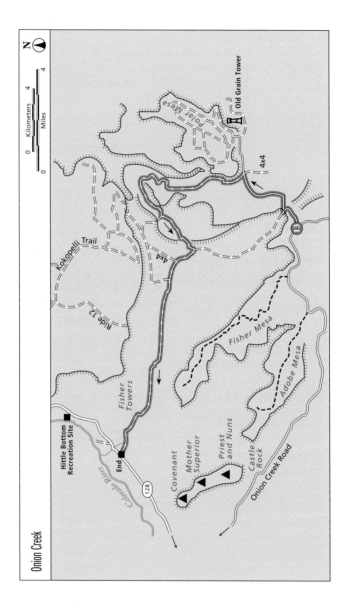

Onion Creek

Road. GPS: N38 43.236' / W109 20.580'. The end trailhead has camping available. Now backtrack 5.9 miles south on UT 128 and turn left onto Castleton Road. Drive 11 miles south and turn left (the paved Loop Road goes right and south). Go 8 miles east (the road turns to gravel) and park at the junction with FR 033. GPS: N38 36.714' / W109 11.745'

The Ride

0.0 Roll northeast on FR 033, which heads downhill and passes a corral.

0.5 An obscure ATV route (FR 4005) goes left. This is a savage shortcut portage into Fisher Valley. Instead, stay on the main road, which climbs a short hill.

4.3 In the middle of this downhill run, turn left at the easy-to-miss Kokopelli Trail marker. Straight continues on to Polar Mesa. Stay left on this road past the two spurs that show up in the next 2 miles. Don't grow numb to the scenery. This ride is just beginning!

7.3 The road bends sharply left. A shortcut goes right, but left leads to a stunning view of Onion Creek Narrows to the west, past an offshoot of Hideout Canyon.

14.3 A killer hill. Didn't believe me, huh?

15.2 Go right as the road forks. Left runs south about 8 miles back to FR 033 and your car. But you'll have to carry your bike up the mesa rim to rejoin the road. And a big chunk of the fun is still ahead.

16.2 Stay left here on the main road as an option of the Kokopelli heads back up Fisher Creek's Cottonwood Canyon.

16.8 Into the Onion Creek drainage we go like lemmings sucked into a whirlpool. Right heads up another way to the Kokopelli Trail (appendix A).

19.8 Can you smell Stinking Spring? The road is deep in the narrows now, and it's not done with the crossings!

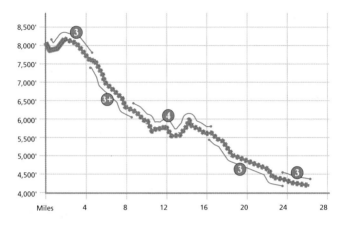

21.2 The foot trail on the right climbs out of the canyon to grant a view of Fisher Towers.

24.7 Keep it pointed downhill as a road enters on the right.

26.2 Draw straws to go get the shuttle car. To wash up in the Colorado, head right up UT 128. A spur left grants riverside access.

14 **Fisher Mesa**

The view of Professor Valley, Arches National Park, Castle Valley, and the Fisher Towers is clouded only by the nagging knowledge that the return climb awaits. The mesa-top ecosystem here is relatively unspoiled and definitely uncrowded—well worth the effort. A singletrack trail now runs along the eastern rim of Fisher Mesa. It skirts the mesa's edges and is definitely the way to go. If you opt to go all the way to the end, keep in mind that it's *all* uphill to get back.

Location: 25 miles northeast of Moab on La Sal Loop Road

Distance: 9 miles out and back with an option to make it a 20.8 mile ride.

Riding time: About 3 hours

Physical difficulty: Strenuous. The ride starts downhill making the return trip an uphill one.

Technical difficulty: Moderate to challenging. The initial downhill is

bouncy, and the climb up to Fisher Peak is on broken ground. The parts between are moderate.

Trail surface: 20.8 miles on four-wheel-drive road that includes packed dirt, eroded and rock-strewn sections, sand, and slickrock

Land status: Manti-La Sal National Forest and BLM

Maps: USGS Mount Waas, Fisher Valley, Fisher Towers

Finding the trailhead: From Moab drive 2.6 miles north on US 191 to UT 128. Turn right, passing Matrimony Spring, and go 13 miles northeast. Turn right onto Castleton Road, drive 11 miles south, and turn left, remaining on Castleton Road (the Loop Road heads right). After driving 2.4 miles, the road forks. Take the main road as it bends left. The road is now called Gateway Road. Continue another 2.4 miles and look for FR 601 on the left. Immediately afterward you'll cross a cattle guard. The trailhead is 200 yards up on the left. If Castleton Road turns to dirt, you've gone 0.3 mile too far. GPS: N38 36.954' / W109 13.416'

Fisher Mesa

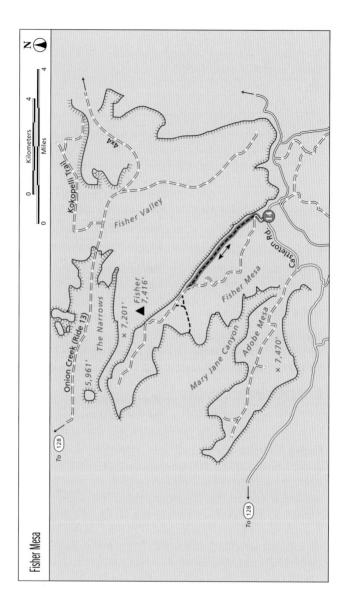

The Ride

0.0 It's probably best to head back down the road, cross the cattle guard, and turn right onto FR 601. You can head north along the singletrack, but it can get confusing. If you opt for the singletrack, just head north and everything will funnel into the proper trail.

0.5 FR 601 passes to the left of a pit toilet. The singletrack bends back, passing the pit toilet structure to join FR 601. If you have a duty to do, this is the place. Whichever way you started, keep on FR 601 (That's a right if you're coming from the privy.)

0.6 A sweeping right-hand turn by a fence starts the dive down onto Fisher Mesa. Yehaaa!

0.8 Stop! Well, you don't really have to stop. You have to turn right and follow the singletrack. The junction is well signed and occurs at the apex of a hairpin left turn. You could opt to bounce down the road and just return on the singletrack. I wouldn't. But it's certainly an option.

4.5 There hasn't been much to this. Just 3.7 miles of glorious descent along a narrow ribbon of trail. The singletrack empties onto the road. If you'd opted to ride the road, your odometer would say 6.9 miles. There's a math lesson hidden in there. Now you can decide if you want to ride 3.5 miles down the road on often-loose rocks to the end of the mesa. If you do, it's easily navigated and isn't even all downhill. So you'll be rewarded with a climb on loose rock in both directions. Still interested? Have at it. It's beautiful. You can also opt to return via the singletrack for a ride totaling 9 miles or return up the loose, rocky road for about 7 miles to get a ride total of 11.4. What? You're asking me? Choose the singletrack. If you must see what the road looks like, do it as a downhill and still return via the singletrack. The most insane thing to do is what we used to do: ride the whole road for 20.8 miles of lung-sucking, leg-destroying fun.

If you do end up going all the way to the end, the last stretch is sandy, but the payoff point has arrived. The rock formations from left to right are Castle Rock, Priest and Nuns, Mother Superior, and the Covenant. Parriott Mesa lies behind the catholic rocks, and the Fisher Towers are the spires to the right across Onion Creek Narrows. Enjoy.

15 **Moonlight Meadow**

This singletrack is primo stuff! It zips through aspen with barely room for the handlebars, then dives down rocky steeps for a ride that will leave finger dents in your grips. The natural hazards of logs and bogs have been slightly tamed with some rerouting and cute bridges that keep usage from ruining this meadow. Yet, with the La Sal scenery and desert views, Moonlight Meadow will etch its way into your personal hall of fame. There's nothing quite like flying through aspens. Watch out for cows.

Location: 23 miles east of Moab off La Sal Loop Road

Distance: 10.1-mile loop

Riding time: About 2 hours

Physical difficulty: Moderate. The ride starts with a gradual 4.9-mile climb, then ends with a brief series of steeps.

Technical difficulty: Moderate to challenging. The climb rates an easy to moderate, but the singletrack throws in many technical tests.

Trail surface: 5 miles on gravel road, 5.1 miles on singletrack. Sections of the road may be washboarded, but it's mostly in great shape. The narrow singletrack carves through a fertile meadow with rocks, loose dirt, roots, and boggy sections.

Land status: Manti-La Sal National Forest

Maps: USGS Mount Tukuhnikivatz, Mount Peale

Finding the trailhead: From Center and Main in Moab, drive 8.2 miles south on US 191 and turn left at the sign for La Sal Loop Road and Ken's Lake. Go 0.6 mile east to the La Sal Loop Road, turn right, and drive 12 miles east and north. Turn right onto gravel Geyser Pass Road and drive 3 miles to a pullout. Here the Trans La Sal Trail crosses Geyser Pass Road and is marked by a trail sign. GPS: N38 28.748' / W109 17.404'

Moonlight Meadow

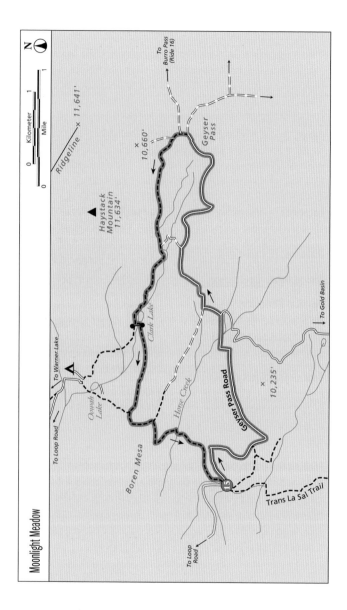

N

0 — Kilometer — 1

0 — Mile — 1

Ridgeline × 11,641'

× Haystack Mountain 11,634'

× 10,660'

To Warner Lake

To Loop Road

Oowah Lake

Clark Lake

Boren Mesa

Horse Creek

Geyser Pass Road

Geyser Pass

To Burro Pass (Ride 16)

To Gold Basin

× 10,235'

To Loop Road

Trans La Sal Trail

The Ride

0.0 Ignore the Trans La Sal Trail for now, and head east up Geyser Pass Road. Stay on this main road until the top of the pass at mile 4.9.

1.2 The view from this sweeping turn takes in much of the desert below.

2.5 Keep left as Gold Basin Road goes right (on its own beautiful out-and-back ride).

2.7 Keep right on the main road as a spur to Boren Mesa heads left.

3.1 Cattle guard.

3.3 Keep right. This spur leads to mile 6.4 of this ride.

4.3 The view on the left foreshadows some of what's to come.

4.9 A sign marks the top of 10,600-foot Geyser Pass. Now it gets fun! Take the left at the triangular intersection, then immediately keep left again at the fork in about 50 yards.

5.0 As the doubletrack road bears right to avoid some scrubby old trees, bear left onto singletrack. It contours across the meadow just above the copse of trees. The tread becomes more apparent before it heads into the aspen groves. Don't stay on the doubletrack as it climbs an insanely steep hill.

5.3 The skinny ribbon of righteousness zips through the aspen. Be careful: The exit from this grove is steep and rocky.

5.7 A boggy meadow offers many cow paths and probably some cows. Be sure to stay right and down to pick up the trail proper. It used to be hard to find, but the trail was given lots of love, making things drier and easier to follow. Thanks! Now might be a good time to mention that you can make a donation to Trail Mix.

6.4 A steep descent leads to the creek. Stay right and don't cross. Crossing leads up to Geyser Pass Road at mile 3.3 of this ride.

6.6 The trail has been rocky and rooty. It now crosses two creek beds, each a technically challenging maneuver.

6.9 This pretty pond is not Clark Lake. View it from the sidehill's perilous perch and continue on.

7.2 This is Clark Lake. Options here are to drop down the switchback as described or swing through the gate for a technical descent to Oowah Lake (see Burro Pass, part of Ride 16).

7.3 After descending to Clark Lake, pass through the gate on the right. Follow the path to the next gate on the left, pass through it, and cross the creek bed. Pick up the trail on the other side.

7.6 Portage this exposed, eroded patch, then follow the singletrack down.

8.3 Turn left up to the top of Boren Mesa at this T junction. Right is to Oowah Lake.

8.6 Turn right and follow the trail markers. The doubletrack leads uphill to Geyser Pass Road and mile 2.7 of this ride.

8.9 The singletrack turns sharply downhill for a technically challenging descent.

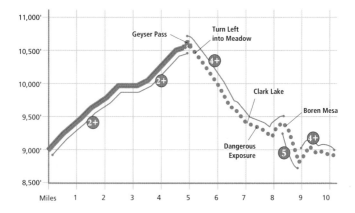

9.2 Keep right at the sign for Boren Mesa.

9.4 Cross the creek and jam it (or more likely portage) up the other side.

9.7 Take the doubletrack to the left.

10.0 Take the right here to return to the trailhead.

10.1 Arrive back at the car, truck, van, or possibly a sport utility vehicle. A moped is right out!

16 **The Whole Enchilada**

You've heard about it. Maybe just in whispers or maybe in some magazine. This is the downhill that goes from the top of the La Sals down to the Colorado River. It's got a mountain pass, high country meadows, expansive valley views, rugged rim riding, brutal climbs, and unimaginably fast descents. It's the Whole Enchilada. For something this big you'll need help in the form of a shuttle (see appendix I). The ride consists of six trails in order from the top: Burro Pass, Hazzard County, Kokopelli Trail Leg, Upper and Lower Porcupine Singletrack, and Porcupine Rim (Ride 17). A description of each section is followed by navigational tips to allow you to ride the sections individually. The real fun comes when you do all six trails, "The Whole Enchilada." The Ride description for this hefty meal follows all the individual trail descriptions.

Location: The top of the La Sals to the Colorado River

Distance: A long, long, long way—25 miles if you must know

Riding time: 3 to 6 hours plus shuttle time

Physical difficulty: Strenuous

Technical difficulty: Challenging. Factor in the length and the technical stuff at the bottom and

the rating jumps to extremely challenging.

Trail surface: Everything Moab has to offer—but without much sand

Land status: Manti-La Sal Nation Forest, BLM, state land

Maps: USGS Mount Tukuhnikivatz, Mount Waas, Mount Peale, Warner Lake, Rill Creek, and Moab

Finding the trailhead: Riding the Whole Enchilada means starting up in the La Sals and ending down by the Colorado River, which means it's a shuttle ride. Appendix I provides the information you'll need to hire a shuttle. For those who want to forgo such a thing, each segment's "Navigation tips" give trailhead information.

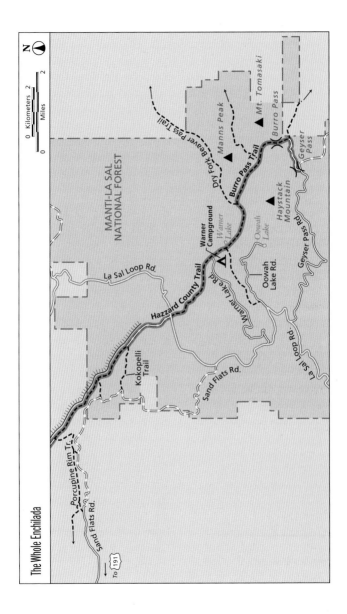

The Whole Enchilada

Burro Pass

This is a true mountain experience. The steep downhill is a radical test of nerves and skill that requires good brakes and "hanging it out" skills. Views take in the desert and Warner and Oowah Lakes. If time and energy permit, the hiking trail from the top of Burro offers views of the region's enormity. Before shuttles, this was a grinding loop. The shuttle drops off at the top of Geyser Pass. Those who are reenacting the classic ride can discover the joy of that whole climb with directions in the "Navigation tips." Keep in mind that hikers and equestrians also use this trail and deserve your respect.

Distance: 5.7 miles point to point (11.4-mile loop option)

Physical difficulty: Strenuous. Very few riders will summit Burro without pushing their mounts. The downhill is arm-numbing . . . but you've only just begun.

Technical difficulty: Challenging. It gets steep. Be careful—fully grown trees could be lying across the trail around any corner, snow may be lurking in the shadows, and the switchbacks are tight.

Trail surface: Besides the initial road in, it's all rugged trail with packed dirt; some loose and rocky sections. Deadfall is always a possibility just after Burro Pass.

Land status: Manti-La Sal National Forest

Navigation tips: If you want to ride Burro Pass by itself, without a shuttle, like we did in the caveman days, you'll need to find the trailhead. From Center and Main Streets in Moab, drive 8.2 miles south on US 191 and turn left at the sign for the La Sal Loop Road and Ken's Lake. This road goes 0.6 mile before ending at the Loop Road (8.8 miles from town). Turn right and follow the La Sal Loop Road to mile 22.2, then turn right onto Oowah Lake Road. Take this to the top (3.2 miles) and park at Oowah Lake. GPS: N38 30.206' / W109 16.335'. Start your journey here at Oowah Lake. Follow trail #037 to Boren Mesa then down a singletrack to Geyser Pass Road (part of Ride 15). Turn left, climb the pass and follow the Whole Enchilada description, then turn left at the 10-mile mark. Follow the brown trail markers to Oowah Lake. It makes for an 11.4-mile loop.

Hazzard County

"Straight'nin' the curves, Flat'nin' the hills. Someday the mountain might get 'em, but the law never will. Makin' their way, the only way they know how. That's just a little bit more than the law will allow." Well, it looks like Roscoe P. Coltrane dun busted the Duke brothers because grass and wildflowers grow from between the rocks that once were gap jumps. When those jumps were launching riders like the General Lee, you could still avoid the hazards. The trail still offers up plenty of adrenaline, but you have to pay. No, you don't need to bribe Boss Hogg. You'll pay with a grind of a climb at the start. Picture Daisy or Bo Duke, depending upon your preference, and you'll be on top of the hill in no time. Once you start rolling down, the mountain is in charge. In the blur that follows, you'll weave back and forth through countless turns, cross three cattle guards, whoosh through a couple groves of aspen trees, fly along the side of a mountain, bounce off and over rocky erosion patches, and be assaulted by scrub brush. Helpful hint: If you decide to stop, wait *off* the trail.

Distance: 2.9 miles point to point
Physical difficulty: Moderate, but your arms will get very tired
Technical difficulty: Moderately challenging
Trail surface: Packed dirt singletrack and eroded rocky singletrack
Land status: Manti-La Sal National Forest
Navigation tips: This is ride number two of the Whole Enchilada, though some folks start here to avoid the climb up Burro Pass. The section ends at the La Sal Loop Road where Roscoe can pick you up and let you ride again, or you can cross the road and keep going down to the third course in your Enchilada meal. To ride this section alone, from Center and Main Streets in Moab, drive 7.8 miles south on US 191 and turn left at the sign for the La Sal Loop Road and Ken's Lake. This road goes 0.6 mile before ending at the Loop Road (8.4 miles from town). Turn right and follow the La Sal

Loop Road 13.7 more miles (22.1 miles from town), then turn right onto Warner Lake Road (FR 0063). Take this up 4.7 miles and turn right. The turn is sharp and leads up to the Hazzard trailhead. GPS: N38 31.529' / W109 16.891'

Kokopelli Leg

So you've just come off Hazzard County. Continue across the paved road and roll on down the dirt road in front of you. It's a steep roll away from La Sal Loop Road. This portion will be the least technical of the whole ride. The world beneath your tires changes from the dirt of the mountains to the rocky road of the desert canyon rims. As you roll on down the road, try to give your arms a rest from the fun of Hazzard County.

Distance: 1.8 miles point to point
Physical difficulty: Moderately easy
Technical difficulty: Moderate
Trail surface: Dirt 2-track and rocky road

Navigation tips: Pop out of the brush and then cross the road from Hazzard County and you're on track (GPS: N38 32.554' / W109 18.741').

Upper and Lower Porcupine Singletrack (UPS and LPS)

Not much to say here. Just your ordinary ribbon of trail dancing with one of the most famous canyon rims in mountain biking. It's pretty nice.

Distance: 2.3 miles point to point
Physical difficulty: Moderate
Technical difficulty: Challenging
Trail surface: Slickrock, ledges, and singletrack over stuff you'll find in a juniper forest
Land status: BLM
Navigation tips: There's a point on the Lower Porcupine Singletrack

(LPS) where you'll have a decision to make. Left is the regular rim ride. This is the way you probably want to go. You may want to walk the initial drop, but the rim is the way to go. The "Notch" section is serious stuff. Honest. The LPS will put you at mile 3.1 of the Porcupine Rim ride (Ride 17). If you're not on the Whole

Enchilada, you may need to get to a trailhead for Upper Porcupine Singletrack. From the Slickrock Trail (Ride 1), continue up Sand Flats Road 10.6 miles. Turn left and go 0.5 mile to the parking area. A rugged vehicle is advised. (GPS: N38 34.498' / W109 20.801'). The very start of the UPS is on FR 4634 (GPS: N38 33.703' / W109 19.644').

The Ride

0.0 Top of Geyser Pass! Take the left fork. Right heads for the old Sheepherder's loop. This is where the shuttle drops you off for the Whole Enchilada. The shuttle should now point you to the right-hand fork. Left leads to the Moonlight Meadow descent (Ride 15).

1.1 Go left on the road to Burro Pass and start the last—but worst—climb. It should be signed FR 240.

1.4 Just past the sign for Burro Pass is a gate. Cross the gate and immediately turn left. The singletrack begins about 30 feet down the fence line. Yes, the climb continues.

1.9 A meadow offers a brief rest from the technical harrows just endured.

2.4 Burro Pass! A humble trail sign points in two directions. To the right is a hiking path to incredible views. The bike route continues on a breakneck descent down over the lip, straight away from the sign.

4.0 The downhill singletrack continues. The route keeps left at this well-signed intersection.

4.4 Keep right here on Wet Creek Mill Fork trail. Left is the Bear Trail and is for hiking.

5.5 Continue straight through this gate and head past Warner Lake. For those making a loop from Oowah Lake, turn left at this gate and go another 1.4 miles past Oowah Lake to reach Geyser Pass Road.

5.7 Welcome to Warner Lake Campground. Wise riders may choose to check out the primitive facilities there. When done with the facilities, follow the road out of the campground.

6.2 A road forks up and off to the right. Follow this up to your next segment, the Hazzard County trail. Yeee! Haaaw!!

6.3 Trailhead parking for Hazzard County trail, which leaves the parking lot on the northwest corner and heads into the aspens then up, up, and up.

9.3 *Careful*! The La Sal Loop Road pops out at you from the scrub oaks. Cross the road and start down the Kokopelli leg of the Whole Enchilada.

10.0 Three-way intersection. Straight or right both work.

10.3 If you went right at 10.0 miles, you'll need to stay left here.

10.9 The two roads become one again.

11.1 An old doubletrack comes in from the left. It's your cue to look ahead for the Upper Porcupine Singletrack (UPS) to exit to the right. It's signed and in the middle of a gently arcing left-hand turn. If you're letting your arms recover, you'll be going a good speed to see the trail. If you missed it, you'll end up on Sand Flats Road 3.3 miles down from the La Sal Loop Road (12.6 miles from the start at Geyser Pass). If that's the case, turn right and follow the road for 1 mile, then keep left (straight) at the fork and ride another 0.5 mile to a UPS trailhead. If you miss that trailhead . . . well . . . damn, you'll be riding down Sand Flats Road. Last chance. You'll cross up and over a cattle guard. *Stop*! GPS: N38 34.707' / W109 21.510'. A singletrack leads along the fence to the right and will T into the Porcupine Singletrack. Turn left and continue. If you missed your chance at the cattle guard, then you'll be tired enough to actually see the classic Porcupine Rim Trailhead farther down the road. But then you'll have a hefty climb to get back to Porcupine Rim proper.

13.4 Join the original Porcupine Rim Trail (Ride 17) at mile 3.1 of its ride description.

25.3 The Porcupine Rim Trail deposits riders onto UT 128 (GPS N38 36.721' / W109 31.929'). There is parking across the road along with a campground and the Moab Canyon Pathway (Ride 2).

17 **Porcupine Rim**

Next to the Slickrock Trail (Ride 1), this is perhaps the most notorious of Moab's rides. The view from the rim is as breathtaking as the cigarettes whose ads use the same background. It's definitely an E-ticket ride to Moab's original downhill romp. The ride has received mixed reviews; some find it too technical for their taste, but it induces perma-grin for those who like boulder boppin' and ledge droppin' along vertigo-inducing cliff sides. When ridden as a loop, it includes the climb up Sand Flats Road, which can get extremely busy and dusty during the high season, and it returns along narrow UT 128. The Moab Canyon Pathway is slated to connect to Porcupine's exit, allowing safer returns to town. For shuttle information see appendix I. This is the classic Porcupine Rim Trail. You've probably heard of LPS and UPS. That refers to the Lower and Upper Porcupine Singletrack. They are prime examples of Canyon Country singletrack and are described in Ride 16. All three Porcupines are part of the Whole Enchilada.

Location: 10 miles east of Moab

Distance: 15.0 miles point to point with a shuttle or a 31.2-mile loop

Riding time: About 2 to 4 hours one-way; 4 to 7 hours for the loop

Physical difficulty: Moderately strenuous. The first climb is fairly extended, but after 4 miles it's all downhill. As a loop, this is definitely strenuous and often dusty.

Technical difficulty: Challenging. The majority of the ride is solid moderate-to-challenging work up and down ledges on steep, rocky slopes. The singletrack is famous for riding that challenges even elite riders. Cocky riders often take soil samples home along with a serving of crow pie.

Trail surface: 11.7 miles on four-wheel-drive road; 3.3 miles on singletrack. The four-wheel-drive road is full of bedrock steps

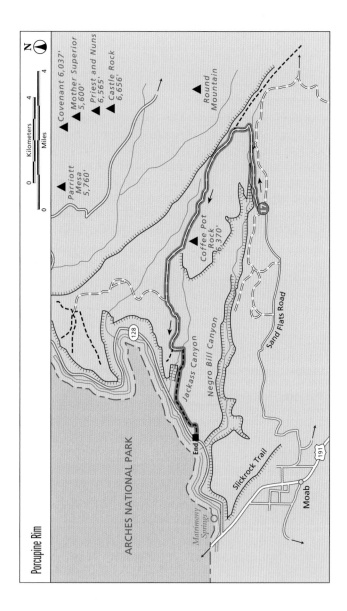

Porcupine Rim

ARCHES NATIONAL PARK

Matrimony Springs

Covenant 6,037'
Mother Superior 5,600'
Priest and Nuns 6,565'
Castle Rock 6,656'

Parriott Mesa 5,760'

Round Mountain

Coffee Pot Rock 6,370'

128

Jackass Canyon

Negro Bill Canyon

End

Sand Flats Road

Slickrock Trail

Moab

191

N

0   Kilometers   4

0   Miles   4

laid down on packed dirt with occasional sandy spots. The singletrack is packed dirt when it's not climbing, dodging, and hopping the encroaching boulders.

Land status: BLM

Maps: USGS Rill Creek, Moab, Windows

Finding the trailhead: From Center Street and Main in Moab, go 0.3 mile east on Center. Turn right onto 400 West and go 0.4 mile, then left onto Mill Creek at Dave's Corner Market. Go 0.5 mile on Mill Creek to a stop sign and continue straight onto Sand Flats Road. (Look for a cemetery on the left as a landmark.) Stay on Sand Flats and pay the appropriate fee at the gate (bike: $2; car: $5; camp: $10). Continue on this road 7 miles to an information kiosk and three big stock tanks sitting by the road. This is the trailhead. GPS: N38 34.911' / W109 25.007'. The road is dirt from mile 4.0 onward and gets washboarded, but it is drivable in a passenger car. The trailhead has a pit toilet. There is no running water, and parking is limited, so leave room for others. Overflow parking is available 0.1 mile back toward town. An alternate trailhead requiring a high-clearance vehicle is 2 miles farther up the road. GPS: N38 35.088' / W109 23.230'

The Ride

0.0 From the trailhead registration box, head down the trail, left from Sand Flats Road.

0.2 Stay right. The spur to the left heads along the rim of Negro Bill Canyon and connects to Sand Flats Road 2 miles west of this ride's trailhead.

1.5-6 Stay right and up as a spur peels off to the left.

1.5 Stay on the main road. The road joining from the right is from the high-clearance portion of Sand Flats Road.

2.4 This transition is pretty tricky as the route dips into the ditch then, presto-chango, it climbs out.

3.1 Look off to the right for the first views of Castle Valley. The Lower Porcupine Singletrack (LPS) enters from the right along with the rubber-armed Whole Enchilada riders.

3.8 Climb to another viewpoint.

3.9 Some techy steps lead to Gapers Point. The road continues playing tag with the rim for a bit. See the map for the names of all the famous rocks of cigarette-ad country.

4.9 A welcome smooth stretch for 0.2 mile.

5.2 Go straight through this signed four-way intersection.

5.4 Stay right at all the forks from here through mile 7.6. Arrows should point the way.

7.8 Keep left at this signed fork.

8.0 A surprise move out of the sand. Another sand trap lurks ahead.

8.2 The trail heads left at this fork.

8.5 Straight on through the four-way intersection.

9.1 Once again, keep left.

10.7 Cross the slickrock to pick up the road on the same heading. Cairns should help with navigation.

10.8 Left here. The right-hand fork heads to a view of Big Bend on the Colorado River. The trail may be blocked off with sticks, but it makes a nice side trip.

10.9 The road enters the wilderness study area.

11.6 Keep right at this fork where two signs were placed. How special.

11.7 Let's get ready to *rrrrummmmmble*! The singletrack starts here.

12.2 The ride is now in Jackass Canyon, with UT 128 visible below.

12.6 Vertigo-inducing section. To paraphrase famous useless advice, "Just don't look down." Here comes trouble.

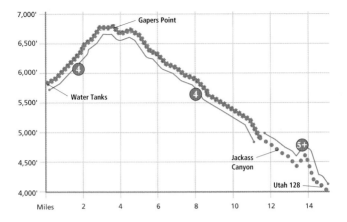

14.4 The trail heads left around a boulder, then down and across the gulch. Definitely technically challenging. Things ease up from here.

14.9 This last hill is a wee bit sandy.

15.0 Welcome to UT 128. Where did you park your shuttle car? Turn left to head back to town if doing a loop. An underpass in Lions Park aids in crossing US 191.

18 **Prospector**

This is kind of like a secret in plain sight. Psst . . . let's do a little prospectin'. Basically that means to meet at the Rock Shop for a quick ride. This is a point-to-point ride with a choice to make in the middle. Taking the high road involves more climbing and requires more bike skills. The low road isn't easy either. A fall here will be a bit like taking a ride down a sandpaper slide. I suggest you don't fall. Since the trail can be ridden in both directions, keep an eye out for traffic.

Location: In town on the north side of Moab

Distance: 1.0 mile point to point

Riding time: 10 minutes

Physical difficulty: Moderately strenuous. The high road is more strenuous.

Technical difficulty: Moderately challenging. The high road is more challenging.

Trail surface: Singletrack over dirt, rock, and sand

Land status: Grand County easement maintained by Trail Mix.

Maps: USGS Moab

Finding the trailhead: Head north from Moab and turn into the dirt parking area just past the iconic Rock Shop. It's 0.7 mile from Center Street on US 191 (aka Main Street). To reach the northern trailhead, keep going another 0.5 mile, just past the Riverside Inn. The trail exits by the Raven's Rim Zip Line Adventure building (435-260-0973). GPS: N38 34.980' / W109 33.166'

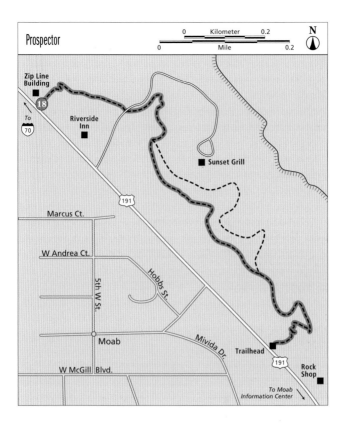

The Ride

0.0 From the northern trailhead, start up the switchbacks heading southward down the trail.

0.2 Cross the Sunset Grill's driveway and keep heading south.

0.4 Time to choose: Are you taking the high road or the low road?

0.8 Whichever path you chose, you are now here.

1.0 Follow the switchbacks down to end at the southern trailhead.

19 **Pipe Dream**

When I wrote the first edition of this guide in the mid-1990s, having permission to build a trail here didn't seem possible. Heck, I wouldn't doubt if folks were considering banning bikes here altogether. It was with some trepidation that I pieced together a route that I called "Beneath the Wires." It was just a patchwork of roads that ran under the power lines. Now thanks to hard work and a forward-thinking town, that patchwork has been replaced with a lovingly built singletrack. Pipe Dream caresses an escarpment of rocks that cradle the southwest side of Moab. The sign at the trailhead encourages . . . no . . . challenges you to ride it "clean." This means to try to ride without putting down your feet. Which is no small feat. Pipe Dream proves that here in Moab you don't need to go far to experience world-class riding. The turns are tight, the climbs steep, and the room for error slim. Good stuff. The suggested direction is from south to north. It's strenuous enough for most in that direction. There are signs at every junction where you can also escape if need be. The Pipeline Road will get you back to the top trailhead. The Pipeline Road was the main part of my Beneath the Wires ride. I remember vividly riding beneath the power lines and feeling an electrical buzz come through my pedals and cleats. Needless to say, I quickly moved along.

Location: In Moab and just south of town

Distance: 4.9 miles point to point

Riding time: About 1 hour

Physical difficulty: Strenuous

Technical difficulty: Challenging

Trail surface: Constructed rock singletrack and packed dirt singletrack

Land status: BLM, state land

Maps: USGS Moab. The junctions are signed with maps by Trail Mix.

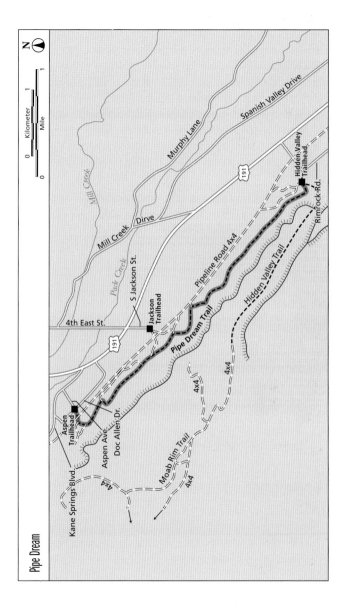

Pipe Dream

Finding the trailhead: Drive 3.9 miles south on US 191 (aka Main Street) from Center and Main Streets. Turn right onto West Angel Rock Road. There should be a small sign pointing the way to the Hidden Valley trailhead, which this trail shares. Go 0.4 mile up the hill to a T intersection and turn right onto Rimrock Road. Go 0.2 mile and turn left to head uphill into the parking area of the trailhead. GPS: N38 31.915' / W109 31.024'. If you're riding from town, you could use the other trailheads: the southern end of South Jackson Street, or Aspen Avenue at Doc Allen Drive.

The Ride

0.0 From the trailhead map sign, head north along Pipe Dream trail. Hidden Valley trail leaves westward from here and is a portage route up to the Moab Rim trail (Ride 20).

0.7 Keep left at this escape route to Pipeline Road.

0.8 Again, keep left.

2.3 Keep left again at this nexus point of trails.

3.3 Continue straight as the trail from the Jackson Street trailhead enters on the right.

3.8 Stay on the left fork. Right heads down to Doc Allen Drive.

4.2 Stay left. Right loops around the water tower and heads back toward where we started or down to Dogwood Avenue.

4.5 Fork in the trail! Right drops down to the Aspen Avenue Trailhead. Left loops over to it. We're taking the left-hand loop.

4.8 We're now heading back the other way. The trail from mile 4.5 joins from the right.

4.9 Cross Pipeline Road and continue about 100 yards to Doc Allen Drive and the Aspen Avenue trailhead. If you want to head back on dirt, Pipeline Road can get you there, or you can get back on the Pipe Dream and go the other direction.

20 **Moab Rim**

Scenery steals the show—massive hunks of sandstone boil up through the desert while a dizzying view simulates a scenic flight over Moab. The difficult sections will have techies drooling while hopping up and diving down. Moab Rim can be ridden as a loop in either direction or as an out-and-back to avoid the long portage through Hidden Canyon. Linking this ride to Pipe Dream (Ride 19) is a fun option.

Location: 2 miles west of Moab on Kane Creek Boulevard

Distance: 12.4 miles out and back

Riding time: About 2 hours

Physical difficulty: Strenuous. The initial climb, which rises 900 feet in under 1 mile, is rideable—honest. Just maybe not all at once. On top, the terrain is much gentler. When ridden as a clockwise loop, this route is moderate with a long, tedious portage.

Technical difficulty: Challenging. This is actually a moderate-to-challenging ride sandwiched between two extremely challenging patches. The climb and descent to and from the rim are extremely technical and steep. The slickrock steps are unforgiving both up and down, but who needs forgiveness?

Trail surface: 10 miles on four-wheel-drive road; 2.4 miles on singletrack (half that if shuttling or doing a loop). It's amazing that four-wheelers can drive this trail! It consists of slickrock, slickrock steps, and some sandy stretches. If ridden as a loop, the Hidden Valley portion that heads through a rockslide is rideable only by an elite handful; it's a portage for the rest of us.

Land status: BLM

Map: USGS Moab

Finding the trailhead: From Center Street in Moab, travel 0.7 mile south on US 191 to Kane Creek Boulevard and turn right. The turn is just before McDonald's. Go 0.8 mile and stay left through this "Dangerous

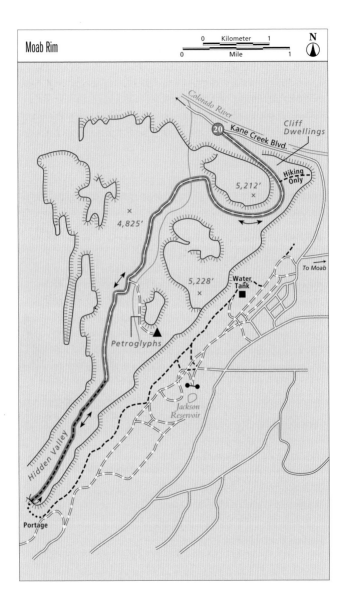

Moab Rim

Colorado River

20 Kane Creek Blvd.

Cliff Dwellings

Hiking Only

5,212'

To Moab

4,825'

5,228'

Water Tank

Petroglyphs

Jackson Reservoir

Hidden Valley

Portage

0 — Kilometer — 1

0 — Mile — 1

N

Intersection" on Kane (it appears to be a left turn). About 3.5 miles from Center Street (2.8 miles from McDonald's), look for the trailhead on the left. It comes up pretty suddenly. The trailhead has two drives in. The second is better for passenger cars. There is a pit toilet at the trailhead. To bike to the trailhead from town, go south on 100 West and turn right onto Williams Way. Go 4 blocks and turn left onto 500 West. Pedal 0.4 mile to Kane Creek Boulevard. Turn right and go 2.7 miles to the trailhead. This way is shorter and sees less traffic. GPS: N38 33.541' / W109 34.965'

The Ride

0.0 From the trailhead registration box, follow the "road" up the slickrock ramp.

0.4 Swing around a quick switchback here as the rock runs out. Pick up the road again on the next fin.

0.9 Up on top. That was the tough part! Walk to the edge, and enjoy the view while catching your breath or administering CPR to your riding partners.

1.1 The road forks; keep right. Left goes to another viewpoint.

1.6 Roll down and up the slickrock softened with sand. The orange sand is laced with black cryptobiotic crust. The huge rock formations are ancient sand dunes.

1.8 Keep right at this fork. Left is an extremely sandy route that is fun but not on a bike.

1.9 Cairns mark the way on the slickrock.

2.1 Slickrock play zone.

2.4 Go up and across the slickrock here.

2.7 Find a slickrock ramp down to the road.

2.9 Careful! A couple of technically moderate-to-challenging ledges pop up here.

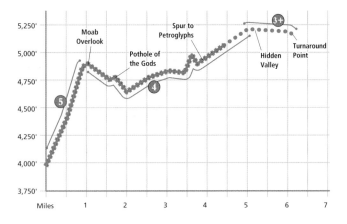

3.5 The Low Road rejoins from the left.

3.7 The route stays right here. But petroglyphs await those who climb the road to the left.

4.4 The road ends but the route continues on singletrack. Follow it straight over the rock that seems to halt progress, then up moderate-to-challenging tread to the ridge.

4.6 The ridge. The trail becomes packed, smooth, and occasionally sandy. This is Hidden Valley trail.

6.2 The trail becomes unrideable. Portage down to the registration box below or turn back, retracing the route to the slickrock stairway and back down to the Colorado River. The trailhead below is for Pipe Dream (Ride 19).

12.4 Arrive back at the trailhead.

21 Pritchett Arch to Gatherer's Canyon

Pritchett Canyon, lined with cottonwoods, winds between towering sandstone walls through a region beset with geologic wonders and prehistoric relics. It costs a buck ($1) to access the trail. Technical treasures lie in wait beneath a picturesque veil for riders to discover. Tears of joy will flow when you think back on every facet of this jewel.

Location: 5 miles west of Moab

Distance: 11.8-mile loop plus a portage

Riding time: About 2 to 3 hours

Physical difficulty: Moderately strenuous. There is one strenuous portion either way you ride this. But the majority is moderate.

Technical difficulty: Challenging. White Knuckle Hill rates as an extremely challenging climb and is only slightly easier as a descent. The more of the singletrack that is ridden, the higher its rating.

Trail surface: 1.9 miles on gravel road; 8.9 miles on four-wheel-drive road; 1 mile on singletrack. The initial ride into Pritchett Canyon consists of sand and cobblestone. Some slickrock snacks await, as well as ledgy climbs and loose, eroded steeps.

Land status: BLM. The first 200 yards cross private property. The owner requires a $1 toll.

Maps: USGS Moab, Trough Springs

Finding the trailhead: From Center Street in Moab, drive 0.7 mile south on US 191 to Kane Creek Boulevard and turn right between the Star Diner and McDonald's. Go 0.8 mile and stay left through the "Dangerous Intersection" on Kane (it appears to be a left turn). About 5.5 miles from Center Street, look for the trailhead on the left. Additional parking is just up the road. There is a small fee per bike. To bike to the trailhead from town, go south on 100 West and turn right onto Williams Way. Go 4 blocks

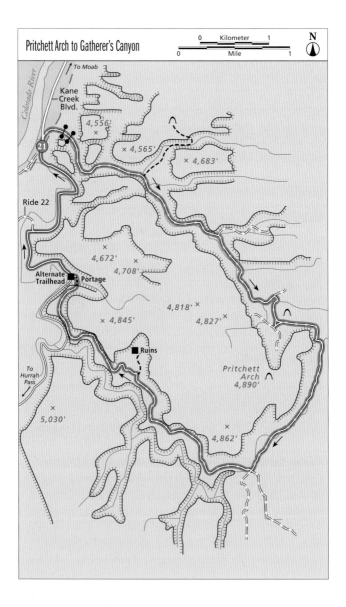

Kilometer

Mile

N

To Moab

Kane
Creek
Blvd.

Colorado River

4,556'
×

× 4,565'

× 4,683'

21

Ride 22

× 4,672'

× 4,708'

Alternate
Trailhead

Portage

× 4,845'

4,818' ×

4,827' ×

To
Hurrah
Pass

× 5,030'

Ruins

Pritchett
Arch
4,890'

× 4,862'

and turn left onto 500 West. Pedal 0.4 mile to Kane Creek Boulevard. Turn right and go 4.1 miles to the trailhead. This way is shorter and sees less traffic. GPS: N38 31.998' / W109 36.065'

The Ride

0.0 After paying the toll, continue up the road past the private campground and through the gate.

0.2 Beware of a technically challenging drop when starting through this sheer-walled canyon. There's a moderate-to-challenging bypass on the left.

0.4 Choose between a 2-foot hop up onto slickrock or the ramp on the right. Up ahead lie some skull-size stones (aka babyheads) in a bed of sand.

1.6 Stay left and cross the technically challenging wash to continue up the canyon.

2.0 After another rocky spot the trail heads up a steep, technical grade.

2.4 The trail forks; turn right and continue up the same canyon.

2.9 Steep uphill with a technically moderate-to-challenging move.

3.0 Keep left as the trail splits then rejoins.

3.2 Rock patch of 30 yards (moderate to challenging).

3.5 Pedal into an open area, then right. Look for a road that heads up out of the wash on the right. It's easy to miss. If you end up riding on slickrock in the wash, you've gone too far. The steep, eroded road is on the right and climbs sharply to look over the open area.

3.9 The track forks; go right (moderate-to-challenging).

4.0 Have a gander at Pritchett Arch, then turn left at this fork to continue. Surprise! There's another arch from whence the road came.

4.2 Keep right and head up the canyon.

4.4 The view from this bench is worth stopping for if you made it up without pushing. This is White Knuckle Hill, accurately named by jeepers.

5.7 The route passes spur roads to Pritchett Arch on the right.

6.1 Standing at the crossroads. Turn right. Straight heads to Kane Canyon Rim and is the return loop option for the Behind the Rocks Trail (Ride 24), which lies to the left.

7.0 The tread is ledgy, broken rock.

8.2 The track forks; go left. Right heads to an archaeological site.

8.5 Start the singletrack and follow cairns around the cliff side. A good portion is rideable, but portage places occur frequently. When above the creek in Gatherer's Canyon, keep following the cairns while looking for the most environmentally friendly way down. This area has taken abuse from people picking their own path. Please be patient and follow the cairn-marked trail. This section is the "no cost" option for Ride 24.

9.5 Turn right onto Kane Creek Boulevard (aka Hurrah Pass Road), climb this lovely hill, then coast back to the car.

11.8 Arrive back at the trailhead.

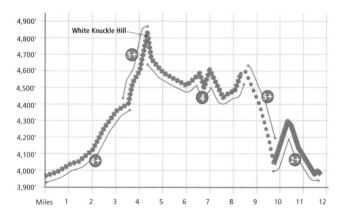

22 **Amasa Back Network**

The insanely steep initial descent of this locals' favorite will test technical skills down and up, while the following climb tests willpower. An extremely technical singletrack creates a loop option. Retracing the route downhill, however, is a rocky, fast-paced frolic. Life should be full of such choices. Speaking of choices, the singletrack revival in Moab has been busy here. Dreamers cranked up a rugged four-by-four trail then explored the rock a bit and imagined wild, twisting, edge-clinging singletrack high above those that dwell below. Welcome to the dream. Rockstacker, Jackson, HyMasa, and Captain Ahab all bring flow to this rock of ages. The classic ride, described here, follows the four-by-four route called Cliff Hanger and serves as access to the singletracks described afterward.

Location: 5 miles west of Moab

Distance: 8.8 miles out and back or a variety of loop options

Riding time: About 2 hours

Physical difficulty: Strenuous. The initial climb and especially the final climb back out are steep. Once on top, the route becomes fairly moderate.

Technical difficulty: Moderate to challenging. The first descent is very technical, and the climb up the other side tosses in some tough spots. Once on top there's a bit of smooth riding. But the whole route demands attention.

Trail surface: Four-wheel-drive road with tons of singletrack options on slickrock, dirt pack, and ledgy bedrock

Land status: BLM

Maps: USGS Moab, Gold Bar Rim

Finding the trailhead: From Center Street in Moab, drive 0.7 mile south on US 191 to Kane Creek Boulevard and turn right. The turn is just before McDonald's. Go 0.8 mile and stay left through this "Dangerous Intersection" on Kane (it seems like a left turn). The trailhead is on the

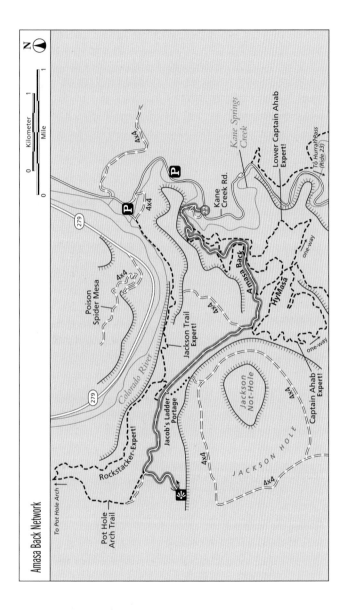

Amasa Back Network

right 0.7 mile after the road turns to dirt at mile 6.3. An alternative trailhead is back 0.7 mile where the road turned to dirt. To bike to the trailhead from town, go south on 100 West and turn right onto Williams Way. Go 4 blocks and turn left onto 500 West. Pedal 0.4 mile to Kane Creek Boulevard. Turn right and go 4.1 miles to the trailhead. This latter way is shorter, sees less traffic, and makes the "dangerous intersection" slightly safer. If you bike from town, you don't have to stop at the trailhead. GPS: N38 31.998' / W109 36.065'

Amasa Back (Classic Ride)

The classic ride, described here, follows the four-by-four route called Cliff Hanger and serves as access to the single-tracks described later.

Distance: 8.8 miles out and back
Physical difficulty: Strenuous. The initial climb and especially the final climb back out are steep. Once on top, the route becomes fairly moderate.
Technical difficulty: Moderate to challenging. The first descent is very technical, and the climb up the other side tosses in some tough spots. Once on top there's a bit of smooth riding. But the whole route demands attention.
Trail surface: Four-wheel-drive road on slickrock, dirt pack, and ledgy bedrock

The Ride

−0.5 Take a right from the parking area and head up the dirt road.

0.0 The signed Amasa Back trail dives off the road to the right. Hang it out and grab the brakes for this Mr. Toad downhill! A section of the HyMasa Singletrack bears left and heads down in a bit-more-sane fashion.

0.1 A 3-foot drop. Careful!

0.2 The bottom of the initial descent can be confusing. The trail leads to a wash and immediately crosses over to begin the climb. It reaches an old gate in about 20 yards. Trails leading up and down the wash are not official. Hike them if you wish to explore.

0.4 Stay on the four-by-four road as Captain Ahab deposits riders on the left. Ahab is a one-way trail. Do not enter.

0.5 Keep right and begin climbing through a series of switchbacks.

0.6 Look for HyMasa on the right for a less technical way up. It will cross a couple more times if you change your mind.

0.8 The brief respite from technical tests is over. Crank into moderate-to-challenging riding.

1.7 Stay right on the road. Left is called "Midline" and connects to the Lower Captain Ahab and HyMasa trails.

2.0 Upper Captain Ahab and HyMasa leave the road to the left.

2.1 After reaching the ridge, the road descends to this fork. The main route stays left. Right is a 0.7-mile jaunt to Buzzards Bluff. It's sandy, but the view of the Colorado and Poison Spider Mesa is worth a look if you have the energy.

2.3 That's Jackson Hole visible off the cliff to the left. Two significant drops in the next 0.1 mile each earn a technical rating of challenging. The second drop has a moderate-to-challenging rating, but it runs precariously close to the cliff's edge.

2.9 Keep on the main road through the next two spurs. The first leads left to Jacob's Ladder (Jackson Hole: Ride 23). The second is a loop option for this ride. It's extremely challenging, has exposure, and deposits riders in Kane Creek, not far from the lower trailhead. It's called Jackson Trail or Jackson's Singletrack.

3.4 Decision time. The trail forks. Right leads to Pot Hole Arch singletrack. Go left to finish up the four-by-four road. Seeing as Pot Hole Arch singletrack is described below, this route will continue left. Actually, left has two choices. Farthest left goes to the rim. The other basically goes along the singletrack. So, let's go to the rim.

3.6 Left continues to the rim. Right heads to Pot Hole Arch.

4.4 The rim. The overlook provides views of Jackson Not Hole and the potash plant. The Jug Handle Loop (Ride 33) is visible as it starts along the river. To explore the expansive Amasa Back portion of this rock, return to mile 3.6 and wander along the other forks. Don't crush the cryptobiotic crust. Ride only on the rock. Check out Pot Hole Arch while you're up here.

8.8 Retrace the above route and arrive back at the trailhead.

HyMasa

Named in memory of Moab local Jonny Hymas, this singletrack opened in 2014 as a bike-friendly alternative to riding the Cliff Hanger four-by-four road. It can be ridden up or down and gives a less-technical option versus the ledges of the classic route.

Distance: 2.3 miles point to point

Physical difficulty: Moderately strenuous

Technical difficulty: Moderately challenging, easier than the jeep road

Trail surface: Slickrock, packed dirt, and broken rock

Navigation tips: Look for a section of this trail at the 0.0 mark for an easier way to start the trail. It then rejoins the four-by-four road at 0.25 mile. Look for it again on the right. It will cross the four-by-four road 3 times and ends at the top of Upper Captain Ahab (GPS: N 38 31.541' / W 109 36.342').

Pot Hole Arch

You'll never guess where this leads you to. After all the technical climbing you've done to reach this trail, it will seem tame by comparison. Don't worry. You're not getting off that easy here. This singletrack is just less technical and less physically demanding than the rest of the stuff up here.

Distance: 1.9 miles point to point
Physical difficulty: Moderately strenuous
Technical difficulty: Moderately challenging
Trail surface: Singletrack and slickrock
Navigation tips: Pot Hole Arch singletrack makes a good loop with Rockstacker for those with the lungs, skill, and nerve for it. If you aren't feeling like Rockstacker is your thing, rest assured that riding Pot Hole Arch back is a new challenge as well. If you do take Rockstacker, know that, if you aren't taking Jackson Trail, you'll have a gnarly climb to get back to the main Amasa Back trail (GPS: N 38 31.872'/ W 109 38.359').

Rockstacker

The name could make you think of a Zen-like activity—calmly stacking rocks. Well, you'll need to enhance your calm to ride it well. Twists and turns with exposure, all for expert riders. It connects Pot Hole Arch singletrack to Jackson Trail. If you don't want to dive down Jackson, I don't blame you. You can still escape that fate at Jackson by turning south (right) to get back to the main Amasa Back trail.

Distance: 1.6 miles point to point
Physical difficulty: Moderate from west to east. It's a strenuous climb back to the four-by-four road if you opt out of Jackson.
Technical difficulty: Extremely challenging
Trail surface: Singletrack and slickrock
Navigation tips: Ridden as a west-to-east connecter of Pot Hole Arch singletrack to Jackson Trail singletrack. Be careful. There is exposure here. Know your ability and ride accordingly (GPS: N 38 32.537'/ W 109 38.450').

Jackson Trail

While definitely a thriller, there's no time for moonwalking this singletrack. First, don't ride down this if you aren't ready for what awaits. Add the very real exposure to this tight, cliff-hugging descent and you'll need all your skills.

Beware also of people walking their bikes. Know your abilities and walk yours too if necessary. Wise people say that acknowledging your limits is the first step to expanding them. I have to tell you about the trail. I have to warn you that the dangers here are real. Sure, all the trails in the book have danger associated with them . . . but it's pretty palpable here.

Distance: 2.1 miles point to point
Physical difficulty: Moderately strenuous
Technical difficulty: Extremely challenging
Trail surface: Slickrock and singletrack. Sometimes loose and rocky, sometimes steep and ledgy, sometimes exposed.

Navigation tips: The end of the trail can be wet. While not listed as officially one-way, it's designed as a downhill, and going up is just as hazardous and could cause trouble. Ride it as a downhill (GPS: N 38 31.762'/ W 109 37.746').

Captain Ahab

Have you spent your whole life hunting an elusive singletrack that's fast, fun, technical, and even a bit exposed? Not a long downhill. A singletrack that's a lot of downhill but is broken up by some climbing. One that is "one-way" to avoid human surprises. A trail made specifically with mountain biking in mind? You won't have to get a boat and a harpoon. It's right here!

Distance: 4.3 miles point to point
Physical difficulty: Strenuous
Technical difficulty: Extremely challenging
Trail surface: Singletrack and slickrock, broken rock, ledges
Navigation tips: Ahab must have the blues. That's the dash color used to blaze the way over the rock. It's reached in two places. To ride the entire trail, look for it just before the 2.0-mile mark of the main Amasa Back trail. The midpoint can be reached by a connector that leaves the Amasa Back trail 1.7 miles from that trail's start. It's one-way and deposits riders at the 0.4-mile mark of

the main trail, before it crosses over the creek to ascend to Kane Springs Road (GPS: N 38 31.062'/ W 109 36.817').

"Towards thee I roll, thou all-destroying but uncon-quering whale; to the last I grapple with thee; from hell's heart I stab at thee; for hate's sake I spit my last breath at thee."

—Captain Ahab in *Moby Dick*,
Herman Melville

23 **Hurrah Pass Trails**

The Hurrah Pass rides offer mild terrain under the tires amid dramatic canyon scenery. From the pass Canyonlands National Park and the Colorado River are seen dissolving into the southwest, while the evaporative ponds of the nearby potash plant are reminders of the outside world in a land of solitude. Dead Horse Point and Island in the Sky rise farther to the west, with the Jug Handle Loop (Ride 33) just across the river. The Jackson Hole and Chicken Corners routes continue over the pass.

Location: 5 miles west of Moab on Kane Creek Boulevard

Distance: 19.4 miles out and back or 29.6 miles when ridden from Moab

Riding time: About 3 to 5 hours for Hurrah Pass

Physical difficulty: Moderate for Hurrah Pass. The other rides are epically strenuous.

Technical difficulty: Moderate. Jackson Hole rates as challenging.

Trail surface: Gravel, sometimes ledgy, road. Jackson Hole has sand, slickrock, and a grueling portage.

Land status: State land and BLM

Maps: USGS Moab, Trough Springs Canyon, Shafer Basin, and Gold Bar Canyon

Finding the trailhead: From Center Street in Moab, drive 0.7 mile south on US 191 to Kane Creek Boulevard and turn right. The turn is just before McDonald's. Go 0.8 mile and stay left through this "Dangerous Intersection" on Kane (it seems like a left turn). The trailhead is on the right just as the road turns to dirt at mile 5.6. GPS: N38 31.998' / W109 36.065'. An alternate trailhead is 3.2 miles farther down the road. But if you're riding this, you probably don't mind an extra climb and won't want to use the alt trailhead. To bike to the trailhead from town, go south on 100 West and turn right onto Williams Way. Go 4 blocks and turn left onto 500 West. Pedal 0.4 mile to Kane Creek Boulevard. Turn right and go 4.1

Hurrah Pass Trails

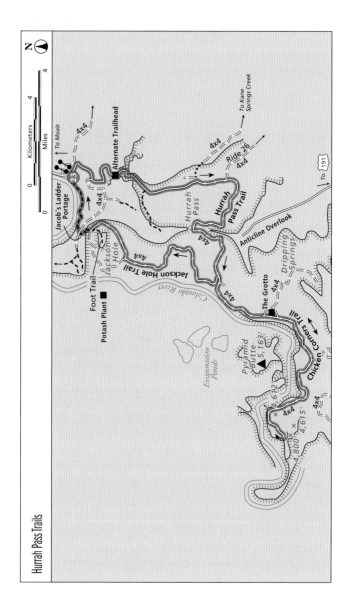

miles to the trailhead. This way is shorter, sees less traffic, and makes the "Dangerous Intersection" slightly safer. If you bike from town, you don't have to stop at the trailhead. Just pick up the ride at the 0.0 mark and keep heading up the road.

Hurrah Pass

The route runs beneath Hatch Point and the rim of Kane Springs Canyon, then clings to the side of the canyon as it winds up to the notch that is Hurrah Pass. The trouble with this ride is that it's often given as a beginner ride. While a lot of the ride is on a dirt road, it's far too long and has way too much climbing for a beginner. Moab now boasts many trails that are much better to introduce someone to mountain biking. This road is often driven by ATVs, rugged SUVs, and four-by-fours, making a ride here a dust-breathing experience. It has its place and time, but it's really not suitable to introduce folks to the joys of biking.

Distance: 19.4 miles out and back.
Physical difficulty: Moderate. Two climbs on the way out and one coming back are strenuous. Good climbers will find this ride easy, and nonclimbers will swear it's strenuous.
Technical difficulty: Moderate. Tight corners can be tricky at speed on the ride back, and the rocky sections occur on steeps.
Trail surface: 19.4 miles on gravel, sometimes ledgy, road
Navigation tips: Simply stay on the road. There isn't any shade and there can be lots of dust on a busy day.

The Ride

0.0 From the parking area turn right and head up the dirt road.

1.2 The Amasa Back trail departs to the right. About 200 feet up on the right is a large cube of rock with petroglyphs on each side. The canyon below here also has many samples of rock art.

1.6 The hill tops out and begins a fast descent with a couple of sharp hairpin turns.

2.2 A reliable spring drips off the left canyon wall.

2.3 Gatherer's Canyon heads off to the left. It is the portage point of the Pritchett Arch route (Ride 21).

3.2 Alternate trailhead parking.

4.2 Keep left as a spur right heads up an extremely technical mine road. True explorer types use this as a return from an Amasa spur (Ride 22). The upcoming spurs on the left head to old mines. Stay on the main road.

6.4 The road crosses the sandy bed of Kane Springs Creek.

6.7 Stay on the main road as the Kane Springs Jeep road leaves to the left (see Ride 26).

8.4 The climb turns tight corners and gets steeper and more technical. The right-hand spurs lead to overlooks of the valley just traveled in.

9.5 When you cross a cattle guard, you'll know the top is near.

9.7 Hurrah Pass summit. Passengers who aren't continuing to Chicken Corners, Jackson Hole, Lockhart Basin, or any points between should retrace the route home.

19.4 Arrive back at the trailhead.

....

Jackson Hole

Jackson Not-Hole and Amasa Rock dwarf bikers as they attack painful climbs and sandy washes spaced among mushroom-like rock formations in the old riverbed. At one point the trail sneaks beneath a gargoylesque passage of rock in Jackson Hole, which was once the path of the Colorado River. The portage up Jacob's Ladder has riders zombie-stepping up 400 feet on a narrow winding path made of packed rocks. The backside of Hurrah Pass is a fast, bone-jarring, white-knuckle descent, and Amasa Rock offers still more downhill choices. This is a great day of riding for the rider that likes to log miles and lug their bike up a cliff.

Distance: 22.5-mile loop. It's an additional 12.8 miles from Hurrah Pass.

Physical difficulty: Strenuous. There are some downright painful hills on this jaunt, and the Jacob's Ladder portage is like backpacking a bike up a skyscraper in a cramped stairwell. Amasa Back adds two more hill climbs, the last of which is very steep.

Technical difficulty: Moderate to challenging. The ride to Jacob's Ladder isn't overly technical. The shake, rattle, and roll downhill from Hurrah Pass is jarring, and Jackson Hole is sandy. Amasa Back demands a lot of off-the-saddle riding.

Trail surface: Gravel and four-wheel-drive road; plus a portage. The Jackson Hole portion mixes sand and broken rock. The rock gets smoother on Amasa Back but is still ledgy.

Land status: State of Utah and BLM

Navigation tips: From the top of Hurrah Pass (9.7 miles), point the tires downhill and hang on. Turn right (12.1 miles) on the road in the dry wash. It's marked with a sign for the Base Camp Adventure Lodge, which also has camping available. Crucial turn (16.6). Turn back to the right and out of this wash. The road continues ahead, but it's longer and sandier. If you don't believe me, make sure to loop around the monolithic rock (which I took the liberty of calling Jackson Not-Hole back in 1997). Turn right onto this spur (18.4) and rig up for Jacob's Ladder (18.6). At the top of Jacob's Ladder, follow the road under the power lines away from the edge. At the T intersection (18.8) turn right. See Amasa Back, Ride 22 (mile 4.0), for a singletrack option. GPS: N38 31.998' / W109 36.065'.

Chicken Corners

Rumor has it that this ride's name stems from guides who enjoyed scaring people around the turns that skirt cliffs above the Colorado River. Thanks to our wonderfully

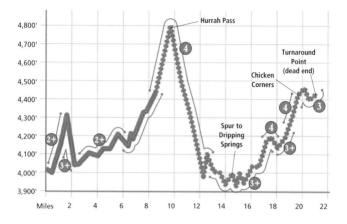

protective government, the road has been "fixed" to give more room. Up-close views of Pyramid Butte and into Canyonlands National Park are great. This is a long affair, so plan accordingly. Lockhart Basin, a multiday adventure, is accessed from this route.

Distance: 42.0 miles out and back. It's 11.3 miles from the top of Hurrah Pass to the turnaround point.

Physical difficulty: Strenuous. The ride features 3 solid climbs, but the main reason for this rating is the overall length.

Technical difficulty: Moderate. The downhills are fast with a few ledges and tight corners that demand respect!

Trail surface: Gravel and four-wheel-drive road. The downhill side of Hurrah Pass starts with bedrock drops followed by craggy cobblestones. Farther down, the road crosses several rough washes.

Land status: BLM

Navigation tips: From Hurrah Pass (9.7), head down the back side of the pass. Keep on the main road as the descent bottoms out where the Jackson Hole route turns right (12.1 miles). After climbing from the Jackson's turn, the road immediately descends again. When it hits the wash, look for a road scraped out of bare bedrock climbing to the right. Take this road. Missing this turn adds some sand, but it reconnects farther down the line.

Keep right as the spur to Dripping Springs goes left (14.2 miles). Stay right past the road to Lockhart Basin (16.5 miles), a nice multiday ride that doesn't require permits. Chicken Corners interrupts (21.0 miles). After skirting around the skinny corners that gave the trail its name, the road finally comes to a dead end. Turn around and find a rhythm for the return grunt.

24 **Behind the Rocks Trail**

This is a mentally tiring ride demanding constant concentration. The route initially follows a portion of the 24 Hours of Moab bike race course, which is so technical you may wonder what made you pick this trail. But it's a fun ride for those ready for a wide variety of challenges. It also loops well by turning left at mile 13.2 to return via a technically mellow road to Prostitute Butte (see map for options). The sand hill at mile 2.1 can be avoided by using roads from Ride 25 and rejoining this route at mile 4.9.

Location: 13 miles south of Moab

Distance: 19.3 miles point to point or a 28-mile loop

Riding time: About 3 hours plus shuttle; 6 hours for the loop

Physical difficulty: Moderate. The initial climb strikes without a warm-up and is followed by a series of steeps in quick succession. Despite this heart-pounding start, the overall route is downhill.

Technical difficulty: Challenging. The first portion of trail borders on insanity. A huge hill of sand is a challenge

to ride downhill, and many of the washes feature chest-high drops. If you survive that, the ride mellows slightly, still delivering ledges, ruts, rocks, and sand— what true phat heads call phun.

Trail surface: Brutal four-wheel-drive road with deep sand, ledges up to 4 feet high, and the gamut of common obstacles.

Land status: BLM and about 100 yards of private property with a required $1 bike toll (see Ride 21 for a no-cost option).

Maps: USGS Kane Springs Canyon, Trough Springs, Moab

Finding the trailhead: To do this ride as a point-to-point trip, leave a shuttle vehicle at the Kane Creek Boulevard trailhead. From Center Street in Moab, drive 0.7 mile south on US 191 to Kane Creek Boulevard and turn right. The turn is between the Star Diner and McDonald's. At 1.5 miles stay

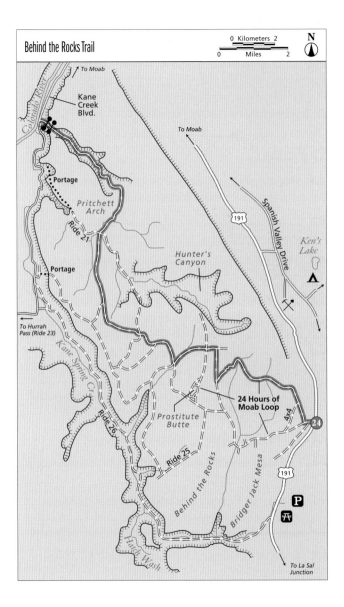

Behind the Rocks Trail

0 Kilometers 2
0 Miles 2

N

To Moab

Colorado River

Kane Creek Blvd.

To Moab

191

Spanish Valley Drive

Ken's Lake

Portage

Pritchett Arch

Ride 21

Hunter's Canyon

Portage

To Hurrah Pass (Ride 23)

Kane Spring Creek

Ride 26

24 Hours of Moab Loop

Prostitute Butte

Ride 25

Behind the Rocks

4x4

24

191

Bridger Jack Mesa

P

To La Sal Junction

Hatch Wash

left through the signed "Dangerous Intersection" on Kane Creek Boulevard (it appears to be a left turn). About 5.5 miles from Center Street, look for the trailhead on the left. Leave the shuttle vehicle here and retrace the route back to US 191. Turn right and drive 12.4 miles south on US 191. Just after climbing a hill and passing mile marker 113, turn right onto a dirt road. Park here. This same trailhead is used for Ride 25. It's easy to miss if you're driving at normal highway speeds. GPS: N38 25.275' / W109 25.971'

The Ride

0.0 From the parking area, pedal west down the main road. Many faint spurs split off right and left, but the main road is obvious.

0.4 The road forks; go right. (Left is the route for Ride 25, Prostitute Behind the Rocks.)

1.3 Stay on the main road. A hard-to-see spur goes right and down to US 191.

1.7 Turn left following the main road. The track becomes sandy and eroded as it runs along the edge of a wilderness study area. A spur road on the right heads into the study area and is off-limits to bikes.

2.1 This huge sandhill downhill is the reason to pedal this ride east to west.

2.5 A dangerous wash-drop lies ahead! With but one gentle stretch, the next 2 miles are very technical.

4.9 Turn right. This brief section is shared with Ride 25.

6.3 A crossroads; go straight. Another steep reason to ride from east to west lies ahead.

7.3 Turn right onto the main road to Pritchett Arch, then immediately right off the road. The route heads uphill, then edges along the rugged hillside.

8.6 Turn right here. Missing this turn leads to the road used in the loop option mentioned at mile 13.2.

9.9 After dropping down this near-cliff pitch, turn right. The roads to the left head back to the main, less technical road used in the return loop. Simply stay on the easily navigated main road, avoiding any spurs.

11.0 Drop over several bedrock ledges and enjoy the technical run in Hunter's Canyon.

13.2 At a well-used intersection, turn right toward Pritchett Arch (Ride 21). Straight goes to Gatherer's Canyon, and left heads back to Prostitute Butte for a nice, long loop.

15.0 Top of White Knuckle Hill. Hang on for a totally gnarly descent, dude.

15.3 The road forks. Go right to stay on the main route. Go left if you want to visit Pritchett Arch (Ride 21) and eventually portage down to Kane Creek Boulevard (a connector road rejoins this route at mile 15.5).

15.6 Drop down yet another extremely steep hill and turn left.

16.8 Keep left here as a spur climbs to the right.

17.6 Cross the wash.

18.6 Keep rolling through basketball-size cobblestones (aka babyheads), and hop a couple of ledges.

19.2 Toll gate. Cross the gate and pay the $1 toll at the next gate. Now go find your shuttle vehicle.

19.3 Arrive at the Kane Creek Boulevard trailhead.

Option: Historically the route for the 24 Hours of Moab overnight race has been held in this area. It makes use of the Behind the Rocks Trail, Prostitute Butte, and other area roads. Check the map for its route.

25 **Prostitute Behind the Rocks— Prostitute's Behind—or A Nice Butte**

Prostitute Butte boasts two arches, and the technical jaunt out to Hunter's Canyon Rim offers a bird's-eye view of the lonely canyon. The ride then is a bump–and–grind downhill back to the main road. To make this much easier, go straight for Prostitute Butte at mile 4.5. Options exist for the whole family here. For those who like it hard and fast, connect with the Behind the Rocks Trail (Ride 24). The main road runs all the way to Pritchett Arch (Ride 21) for a nice, long shuttle ride. The increase in ATV popularity has made for more sand on the main roads. Waiting to ride after a rain helps pack things down.

Location: 13 miles south of Moab

Distance: 20.3-mile lariat-shaped loop

Riding time: About 2 to 4 hours

Physical difficulty: Moderate. The initial ups and downs are long and gradual; later hills are shorter and steeper. The final thrust to Prostitute Butte is a definite grind. But after that climax, it's a gentle push to a wild downhill release. Without recent rain, the sand makes the ride aerobically tougher. If length isn't important, heading straight for the Prostitute at mile 4.5 cuts 8.2 miles off the ride.

Technical difficulty: Moderate. Expect mostly smooth sailing with some small ledges, slickrock, and sand in washes and around the butte.

Trail surface: The gravel and four-wheel-drive trail is mostly hard with intermittent soft, sandy sections. From the butte onward the track erodes into slick grooves and bare rock, then returns to gentle tread for the leg home. Rain

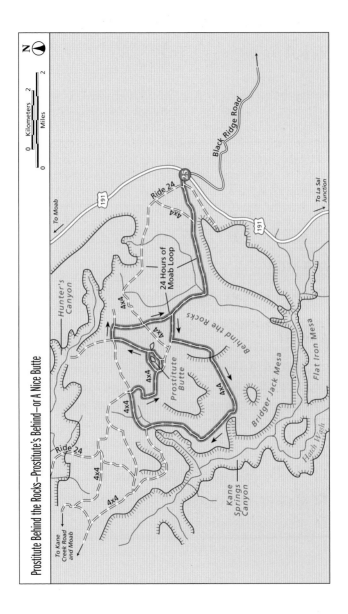

Prostitute Behind the Rocks–Prostitute's Behind–or A Nice Butte

mixed with bovine activity can make the gravel road quite rough but will pack the sand.

Land status: BLM

Maps: USGS Kane Springs, Trough Springs

Finding the trailhead: From Center Street in Moab, drive 13.1 miles south on US 191. Turn right onto a dirt road that appears just after the highway climbs a hill and shortly after mile marker 113. It's easy to miss at highway speeds. A left turn is more easily visible at the same point on the road. If you get to the Kane Springs Picnic Area or the Hole-in-the-Rock House, turn around and try again. Cross the cattle guard and find a place to park. GPS: N38 25.275' / W109 25.971'. High-clearance vehicles can continue to the alternate trailhead 2.3 miles down the road to shave off the final climb.

The Ride

0.0 Leave the parking area on the main dirt road. Head north in the direction of Moab, with US 191 to the right. Many faint spurs split off in all directions, but the main road is obvious.

0.4 The road forks; stay left. To go Behind the Rocks, turn right— it's no fun riding clockwise. The 24 Hours of Moab race loops counterclockwise for its course.

2.3 Keep right, on the main road. This is the alternate trailhead.

2.6 Keep left, on the main road.

2.9 Keep right and cross the soft, sandy wash.

3.0 Follow the sign toward Pritchett Arch and go right.

3.2 Stay on the main road as right-hand spurs go to the sand dunes.

3.6 The sand and rock grab the tires here.

3.7 Sand trap! *Aooga*! Sand trap!

4.0 Keep left. The road right is used on the return trip (mile 16.3).

4.5 As the hill tapers off, a doubletrack leaves to the left. Follow the doubletrack toward Kane Springs Canyon. Remaining on the main road leads straight to Prostitute Butte and rejoins the route below at mile 12.7.

5.6 A spur to the right heads down the slickrock. Take this to hook up with the doubletrack that heads through the small valley. A sand trap mars the start. Do not take the very faint doubletrack to the right (if you even see it).

7.2 The road forks. The left-hand track is more worn, but it's the nearly indiscernible right-hand track you want. Be looking for it and follow it with the canyon on the left.

7.8 Stay right at this sandy fork.

8.7 A cairn marks the right-hand turn at this fork. The canyon views get better and better. The tread now has some slickrock candy and packed dirt.

8.9 A technically moderate-to-challenging rock step.

9.5 Another moderate-to-challenging rock step.

10.2 Crank through the sand and slickrock in this wash and up the other side. The head of the canyon is quite a sight.

10.4 Right back onto the main road. Ignore any spurs.

11.3 Anticipation builds as Prostitute Butte looms up to the right, and you grunt through another sand trap.

11.5 Three-way intersection. Turn right and head up to the butte.

12.7 Turn left, then follow the road all the way around the rock to see the naked beauty of both arches. On the next time around, keep straight as you cross the saddle and join the doubletrack to the north.

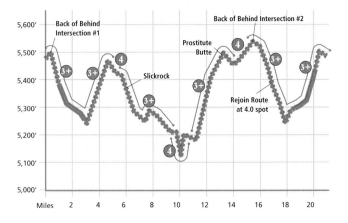

14.2 Four-way intersection. Turn right. Straight goes to Hunter's Canyon and is definitely worth the technical and physical effort. Left heads down to the 11.3-mile point.

14.5 Keep right on the red road. Watch the ruts, then unclamp those brakes as the road races to meet itself at mile 4.

15.5 Stay straight on the main road. Left here runs to the Behind the Rocks Trail (Ride 24), but in the wrong direction.

16.3 The 4.0-mile point. Turn left to retrace the route back to the trailhead. Ahh . . . was it good for you?

20.3 Arrive back at the trailhead.

26 **Kane Springs Canyon**

This is a wet one. Kane Creek usually has an ample flow, and the ride dives right into it. The sand is rideable for the most part, but it gums up drivetrains! The canyon induces claustrophobia with towering, crumbling walls. It's almost a relief when Hurrah Pass comes into view. As a loop with the Pritchett Arch route (Ride 21) and the numerous roads of Behind the Rocks, this ride is extremely exhausting. Take along a good set of tools and nourishment—it's a long way back to civilization and the sand is tough on equipment. Did you pack a chain tool?

Location: 16.2 miles south of Moab

Distance: 20.2 miles point to point. Don't even think of doing this as an out-and-back! A long, clockwise loop is possible with the Prostitute and Behind the Rocks routes (see Rides 25 and 24).

Riding time: About 3 to 5 hours, depending upon creek and sand conditions. Start early if considering the daylong loop, and have a backup plan that includes extra food and extra chain.

Physical difficulty: Moderate. The sand can be exhausting, but the ride runs gradually downhill.

Technical difficulty: Challenging. The cobblestone tread, creek crossings, and sand all demand concentration to maintain the necessary momentum.

Trail surface: 6.7 miles on gravel road; 13.5 miles on four-wheel-drive road. For 9.5 miles the four-wheel-drive road crosses and travels in Kane Springs Creek on cobblestone and sand before becoming hard-packed with some eroded ruts. The gravel road is well maintained.

Land status: BLM

Maps: USGS Kane Springs, Trough Springs

Finding the trailhead: From Center Street in Moab, drive 16.2 miles south on US 191 to the trailhead on the right. GPS: N38 22.883' / W109 27.362'. You'll pass by a roadside rest and the "Hole in the Rock" sign. To do

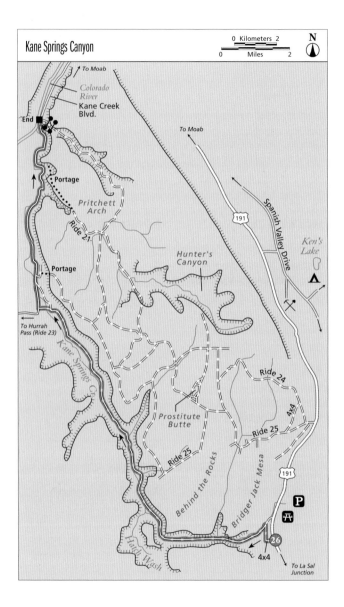

Kane Springs Canyon

0 Kilometers 2

0 Miles 2

N

To Moab

Colorado River

Kane Creek Blvd.

End

Portage

Pritchett Arch

Ride 21

Portage

To Hurrah Pass (Ride 23)

Kane Springs Creek

Hunter's Canyon

To Moab

191

Spanish Valley Drive

Ken's Lake

Ride 24

4x4

Ride 25

Prostitute Butte

Ride 25

Behind the Rocks

Bridger Jack Mesa

191

P

26

Hatch Wash

4x4

To La Sal Junction

this ride as a point-to-point trip, leave a shuttle vehicle at the Kane Creek Boulevard trailhead mentioned in the Hurrah Pass ride (Ride 23) (GPS: N38 31.998' / W109 36.065').

The Ride

0.0 Head away from the highway.

0.1 Turn right on the jeep road and follow it toward Kane Creek.

0.5 The road makes a hard left down to the creek, crosses, and heads upstream. Are you sure you want to do this? It will be just as hard coming back if you change your mind later.

2.3 A spur to the right crosses the creek to another section of trail. It is rideable, but it ends and you'll have to backtrack.

2.8 The road rises above the canyon floor. For the next 7 miles, riders must blast through the creek crossings and the sand between them.

6.3 Hatch Wash enters from the left as the route completes a mile-long bend to the right.

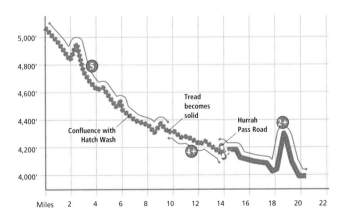

9.5 The tread leaves the sand for higher, harder ground. It might be a good idea to degunk your drivetrain here.

13.5 Turn right onto the gravel road (Kane Creek Boulevard, aka Hurrah Pass Road), and follow it to the shuttle vehicle.

20.2 Kane Creek main parking area. It's 5 miles to Moab from here.

27 Flat Pass

Flat Pass delivers a lot of what the region offers. Petroglyphs and pioneers' inscriptions show the area's popularity through the ages. Views into Canyonlands National Park are nothing short of spectacular, and the immediate surroundings include a canyon with huge, vertical rock walls split in two by a perennial creek lined with greenery. The four-wheel-drive portion starts with ledgy technical tests and finishes with cobblestone and sandy creek crossings. Nothing stirs emotions like a mile of deep sand. Yum. The four-by-four crowd call this trail "Steel Bender." You'll see marks on the rock attesting to the reason for the name.

Location: 10 miles south of Moab near Ken's Lake

Distance: 18.4-mile loop. Leaving a car near the end point saves 7.8 miles of road riding.

Riding time: About 2 to 4 hours

Physical difficulty: Moderately strenuous. The initial climbs are strenuous, but they allow for recovery. Obstacles may make this trail seem aerobically tougher.

Technical difficulty: Moderate to challenging. Paved and gravel roads offer no significant technical challenges, but the four-wheel-drive portion rates a solid moderate to challenging, with challenging patches demanding constant attention.

Trail surface: 9.1 miles on four-wheel-drive road; 1.5 miles on gravel road; 6.8 miles on paved road. The four-wheel-drive road offers lots of slickrock and bedrock ledges. Sand becomes a problem after crossing Mill Creek.

Land status: BLM land surrounded by private holdings and a travel-restricted region

Maps: USGS Kane Springs, Rill Creek

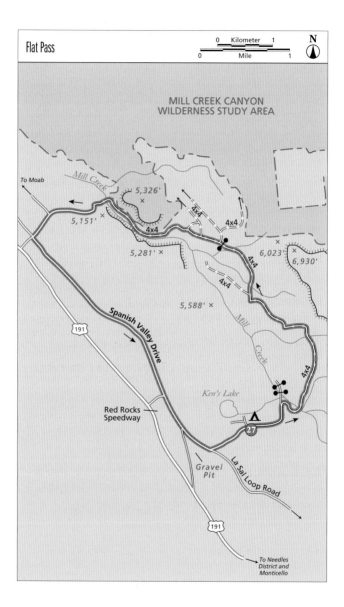

MILL CREEK CANYON
WILDERNESS STUDY AREA

0   Kilometer   1

0   Mile   1

N

Mill Creek

5,326'
×

4x4

4x4

4x4

To Moab

5,151' ×

4x4

5,281' ×

6,023
×

6,930'

4x4

4x4

5,588' ×

Mill Creek

Spanish Valley Drive

191

4x4

Ken's Lake

Red Rocks
Speedway

27

La Sal Loop Road

Gravel
Pit

191

To Needles
District and
Monticello

Finding the trailhead: From Center Street in Moab, drive 8.2 miles south on US 191 and turn left at the sign for the La Sal Loop Road and Ken's Lake. This road goes 0.6 mile before ending at the Loop Road (8.8 miles from town). Turn right and follow the Loop Road 1.5 miles as it bends left past a gravel pit. Turn left onto the paved Ken's Lake access road, then go 0.6 mile and turn left into the parking area. GPS: N38 28.506' / W109 25.602'

The Ride

0.0 From the parking area on Ken's Lake Road, turn left and pedal east on the main gravel road.

1.3 Stay on the main road. A side road going left offers a close look at a man-made waterfall and some petroglyphs.

1.5 After crossing the cattle guard and descending, turn right at a T intersection (the road left enters private property).

1.8 Inscriptions on the rock here deserve a look and mark a "don't-miss" left-hand turn. Cross the creek and follow the road up to the right.

1.9 This slickrock zone can be confusing. Follow the tire marks.

2.1 This technically moderate-to-challenging ascent is a sign of things to come.

2.6 Watch the drop into the wash.

3.3 Enjoy the view west, then follow the trail arrow that points the way. Avoid the old roadbed on the right.

3.6 Stay left where the road splits. Climb out of the wash on slickrock. A series of technically challenging maneuvers awaits as the route switchbacks right. The next mile remains fairly technical.

5.4 Stay right at this fork.

5.5 Another fork; stay left.

5.6 Go straight through this intersection. An arrow points the way (if it has survived the region's world-class sign hunters).

5.8 A nice luge run is interrupted by this sandy turn.

5.9 Climb on slickrock to a left-hand turn at a T intersection.

6.9 A long downhill ends with a technically moderate-to-challenging ascent.

7.0 Pass through the gate and take a left at the next fork.

7.4 Keep on the left side of this slickrock. Look for a rock cairn marking the road.

8.1 Turn left and down, then keep left at this confusing intersection. A technically moderate-to-challenging descent awaits.

8.5 Keep right. The road is riddled with cobblestones and enters the canyon floor.

9.2 Cross Mill Creek. Here comes the sand.

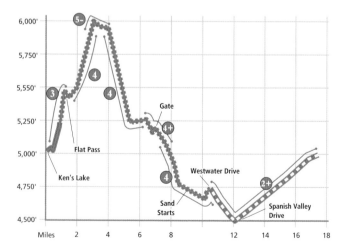

9.7 Cross the creek. Yup, it's still sandy.

9.8 A brief respite from the sand and another creek crossing.

10.2 Solid ground at last. Follow the switchback up and to the left. Anything else is trespassing.

10.3 Climb a steep pitch, past a gate and onto sandy tread again.

10.6 Turn left onto paved Westwater Drive.

11.7 What the . . .? Oh, it's a traffic circle (aka a roundabout). Enter the traffic circle and exit directly across from where you entered to continue on East Spanish Trail Drive.

12.4 Turn left onto Spanish Valley Drive.

16.4 Old Airport Road enters from the right. Stay straight. The road is now the La Sal Loop Road.

17.0 Bear left to stay on the La Sal Loop Road.

17.8 Turn left toward Ken's Lake on the paved access road.

18.4 Loop is complete. Go find the car.

28 The Magnificent 7 and Gemini Bridges Area

Fade in (*dramatic music plays quietly*). . . .

The Trail Mix Committee's concept was to get bikers off the four-by-four roads such as Gemini Bridges. The vision was to improve the recreational experience for all groups. To this end, they pitched "The Magnificent 7" (*music builds*)—a group of trails that would work off the existing trail network to allow rides of epic proportion while also making the parts of such rides available to those less fit (*music reaches a crescendo*). These seven trails: Gemini Bridges, Bull Run, Great Escape, Little Canyon, Gold Bar Rim, Golden Spike, and the Portal stand proud among the giants in a land that . . . OK, *cut*! I'm rambling here. The trails *are* pretty sweet though. Like the Whole Enchilada, the Magnificent 7, aka Mag-7, links together a wide variety of riding in one epic package. The region also adds three other trails to the Gemini Bridges theater: 7-Up, Getaway, and Arth's Corner.

Every intersection near Gemini Bridges Road has a "you are here" map, allowing on-the-fly decision making. Just keep in mind that the map looks flat. Anyone who's ridden Gold Bar Rim (Ride 29) can attest to the fact that it is anything but flat. So keep your fitness level and skills in mind and have fun out there. The Gemini Bridges ride will serve as your exit route unless you're embarking on the herculean feat of Gold Bar, Golden Spike, Poison Spider, and the Portal. You'll want to save enough energy to climb that final hill. While many take shuttles or park at Moab Brands, there are places to park near the actual Gemini Bridges for those who want to start in the middle.

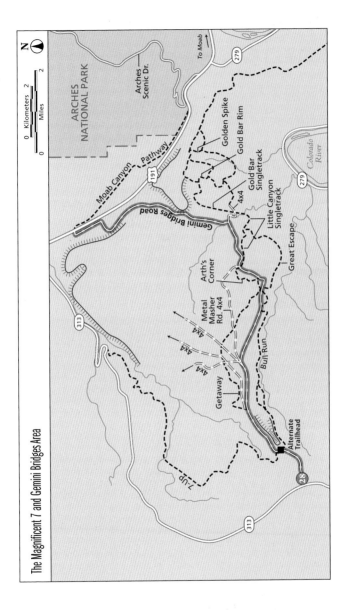

The Magnificent 7 and Gemini Bridges Area

Location: Northwest of Moab around Gemini Bridges

Distance: 26.0 miles in 7 different chunks; 1.3 miles is the shortest reel in this epic film. Gemini Bridges, the region's classic ride, is 11.3 miles point to point.

Riding time: The Mag-7 is a full day. Gemini Bridges takes 1.5 to 3 hours.

Physical difficulty: The whole saga is extremely strenuous. Yet the individual reels can be moderate.

Technical difficulty: Extremely challenging when taken as a whole. However, you can play here all day on moderately easy trails and roads.

Trail surface: Packed singletrack, slickrock, sand, rocks both broken and whole, four-by-four road

Land status: BLM and state land

Maps: Merrimac Butte, Gold Bar Canyon, and The Knoll USGS

Finding the trailhead: From Center and Main Streets in Moab, drive 10.2 miles north on US 191. Turn right into the Moab Brands trailhead. This is the shuttle parking area (or an alternate trailhead for those who like climbing). For the main trailhead, continue about 1.2 miles north on US 191 and turn left onto UT 313. Drive 12.8 miles west on UT 313. Shortly after passing a pump station on the left, look for a gravel road on the left near the top of a hill. It's Gemini Bridges Road. Take it 1.3 miles to the parking area on the right (GPS: N 38 34.921' / W 109 46.581').

....

Gemini Bridges

Gemini Bridges (technically, they are arches) are twin spans over a deep canyon. Biking on the arches has been deemed too dangerous and is no longer allowed. The ride can be dusty, as it is a popular road with four-by-fours and ATVers. Bike shops can help you arrange a shuttle to keep it all downhill. If you're quiet and lucky, you may be rewarded with a glimpse of the endangered desert sheep. The singletrack revival has been busy in this neck of the desert. The Magnificent 7 trails are accessible from the

Gemini Bridges route, allowing you to increase the trail time as you see fit.

Location: 20 miles northwest of Moab

Distance: 11.3 miles point to point with a shuttle and 0.4 mile hiking. Some choose to start at the ride's endpoint for a 15.6-mile round-trip to the bridges.

Riding time: About 1.5 hours without sightseeing time. Plan on a full day to explore.

Physical difficulty: Moderately easy. It's all downhill except for a doozy of a climb at the end. The upper body takes a beating.

Technical difficulty: Moderately easy. Riding at high speed increases the degree of difficulty!

Trail surface: 11.3 miles on gravel road with a few sections of four-wheel-drive track.

Land status: BLM

Navigation tips: Lots of options leave the road and signs with maps will guide you. This road is rideable by almost all ability levels (GPS: N 38 34.921' / W 109 46.581').

The Ride

0.0 Head down the gravel road and hang on as canyon views speed by on the right.

2.7 A four-wheel-drive track goes left to Arth's Pasture. Stay right.

2.9 Another track breaks left to Arth's Pasture. Stay right.

3.6 The Four Arches Trail into Crips Hole goes right. Stay straight on the main road.

4.7 A sign that says "Gemini Bridges" points out this right turn. Gemini twins are painted on the slickrock to blaze the trail. You have to dismount here. You can't ride on the bridges anymore. **Walk** 0.2 mile to the bridges . . . an awesome picnic site. When you're ready, retrace your tracks back to the main road. Turn right onto the main road and continue the descent. Ignore the well-signed spurs and follow the twins.

6.0 The road to Arth's Pasture returns on the left. Stay right.

6.8 Keep right as the other Arth's Pasture road joins up.

7.0 This is the crucial Trigger Road intersection for those who plan on exploring. Bull Canyon's two forks and Trigger's overlook of Day Canyon lie down this road to the left. Stay left to complete the ride described here.

7.6 Turn left after a steep, loose descent. Stay on this main road all the way to the trail's end.

9.3 The hill climb hath arrived.

9.8 After a false summit the real top makes the scene.

11.3 End of the line. Turn right into the parking area. If you didn't bring a car, follow the access directions back to the trailhead, or you could take the Moab Canyon Pathway back to town or even get more riding in at the Moab Brands!

Bull Run

Those of us in the Union call this Bull Run. The Confederacy names things after . . . uh . . . sorry. That's some Civil War material left over from the changing of the Monitor and Merrimac trail (Ride 11). Bull Run is a kick-booty ride. Canyon rim riding, fast, flowing singletrack, and slickrock fun are all part of Bull Run. So is exposure. I'm not talking naked bodies, though you never know what'll happen in the desert. No. I'm talking cliffs that you could fall off of. That rim riding should be done with care and with a good knowledge of your brakes and a willingness to use them. It's an adrenaline-inducing roll in the high desert. What could be better than that?

Distance: 5.1 miles point to point
Physical difficulty: Moderate

Technical difficulty: Moderate. Though one point has exposure on *both* sides.

Trail surface: Slickrock (with yellow dots blazing the way) and packed dirt singletrack
Navigation tips: There are 4 points where you can leave the trail to access the Gemini Bridges trail. The Mag-7 route is to roll from here to Arth's Corner with a stop to hike 0.2 mile to the arches, which are actually bridges. I'd explain the arch/bridge thing, but it's pretty top secret (GPS: N 38 34.920' / W 109 46.566').

Arth's Corner

A short, fun, mostly slickrock connector between Bull Run and the Little Canyon Singletrack. The builders say it's 60 percent slickrock and the rest singletrack. Whatever the ratio, I suggest riding rather than measuring. Arth's Corner is a fun trail and a great idea to help folks better enjoy the region and the sport. The trail is set up for intermediate riders, but beginners riding the Gemini Bridges Road may want to try it out, keeping in mind their abilities. If you are trying slickrock and singletrack for the first time, do yourself a favor and choose caution over bravado. One more tidbit. What's an Arth? Well … the area up here is called Arth's Pasture and the trail in the corner of the area? Work with me here. Anyway, the winding through a desert forest of sorts with junipers and piñons while riding on slickrock is pretty sweet. Oh, you newbies. Follow the painted dots on the rock. It keeps the crust safe (see "Riding Right!" in the introduction).

Distance: 1.5 miles point to point
Physical difficulty: Moderate
Technical difficulty: Moderate
Trail surface: Slickrock and dirt singletrack
Navigation tips: Grab this trail after you hike to the Gemini Bridges. It's on the left just down Gemini Bridges Road where Bridges Spur road joins up. Arth's deposits riders on Metal Masher, a four-by-four option. Turn right toward the south to go back to the lower trailhead by Moab Brands or continue on the Mag-7. If you commit but then change your mind, you'll have to do some backtracking or take the Great Escape (GPS: N 38 35.262' / W 109 42.212').

Little Canyon Singletrack

A moment of silence for Little Canyon Singletrack. The Abominable Sand Monster once called this area home. LCS has slayed the beast. Sure, it's another stellar build with desert forest beauty. Sure smells nice when conditions are right. But let's be real. The scenery is just a bonus. Avoiding the sand is priceless.

Distance: 2.3 miles point to point

Physical difficulty: Moderately strenuous

Technical difficulty: Moderate. I know, right? Moab's trails are tougher than many. This ranks moderate.

Trail surface: Slickrock, and singletrack with ledges to drop off of, dirt, rocks, desert joy

Navigation tips: Remember when I said you had to commit to Mag-7 if you rode Little Canyon Singletrack? Well, you can bail at the start of Gold Bar by hanging a hard left and dropping down the four-by-four trail. The problem is, once you're down there, you'll be slogging through some of that sand we just avoided. It's not too bad. Half a mile at most. Check the Gold Bar Rim description (Ride 29) (GPS: N 38 35.771' / W 109 41.625').

Getaway

This is a great idea—another Gemini-area singletrack that gets folks off the dirt road. This has all the right things to be great. Even green paint blazes on the rock. What it's lacking at the moment is more riders to pack it down. The problem is the competition. Bull Run has a reputation that's tough to beat, and not many folks have enough time to explore all this area has to offer. Thus, less packing for Getaway. What did the Beatles say? "Gettin' better all the time." Don't get me wrong: This is a fun trail, but it isn't Bull Run. That's a good thing. Getaway gives you a different feeling. Another face of the desert. For now, you may want to ride this a day or so after a rain. Oh wow. I just had a thought. Winter?

Distance: 4.4 miles point to point
Physical difficulty: Moderate
Technical difficulty: Moderate
Trail surface: Slickrock and dirt singletrack. The dirt could stand some packing. Thank you to the others that ride the trail and help pack it.

Navigation tips: Keep the flow as you cross the roads, and you'll easily navigate a clean getaway. Getaway connects to Great Escape. Thank you, trail-naming person (GPS: N 38 35.696' / W 109 45.485').

Great Escape

How does Great Escape link to the Magnificent 7? It's an alternative to Arth's and Little Canyon Singletrack. You'll chase away your troubles following the green blazes over the mostly rock trail. Like Steve McQueen, this route doesn't need gimmicks. It oozes cool. Which helps on a hot day.

Distance: 3.5 miles point to point
Physical difficulty: Moderate
Technical difficulty: Moderate
Trail surface: Mostly slickrock with some dirt singletrack

Navigation tips: Connect to Little Canyon Singletrack to loop back to Arth's or to continue on to Gold Bar. Pick the trail up right across from Arth's upper terminus on Gemini Bridges Road (GPS: N 38 35.245' / W 109 42.237').

7-Up

This can be ridden as a downhill, but I can't help thinking that with a name like 7-Up and the fact that it connects to Magnificent 7's trailhead, it's meant for some superhuman riders to make an extreme epic. It's possible to ride from the Lions Park Transit Hub to UT 313 and then to the lower 7-Up trailhead and start your Mag-7 obsession. Extremely epic. It's a fun romp down from the Mag-7 trailhead. Trouble is, now you're out on UT 313. I suggest parking at Moab Brands and either riding up UT 313 and 7-Up or riding up Gemini Bridges Road with Arth's and Getaway, then bombing 7-Up.

Distance: 9.5 miles point to point

Physical difficulty: Strenuous from the bottom. Less so as a downhill.

Technical difficulty: Moderate

Trail surface: Old road parts Frankensteined together with singletrack

Navigation tips: What in blue blazes is this? If you want to climb up this trail, look for the entrance on UT 313 just after the second, gnarly switchback at the top of the hill on the left (GPS: N38 38.673' / W109 43.818').

29 **Gold Bar Singletrack and Rim**

The Gold Bar Rim is trail number four of the Magnificent 7 group of trails. The views are great. But this trail's serpentine route over a huge, eroded slab of white slickrock is the main draw. As an out-and-back ride to the rim, it's fun. As a shuttle route with the Portal Trail via the Golden Spike and preceded by the rest of the Mag-7, it becomes epic. Another option is to hook into the Poison Spider Mesa Trail (Ride 31) and come out that way. The ride to the start from the Moab Brands parking area allows legs to limber up and often draws peak performances from riders. Besides, it's as easy as following the little yellow dots, right? A ride worth its weight in memories.

Location: 10 miles north of Moab

Distance: 12.2 miles point to point to the Portal Trail, then 2.5 miles more to Potash Road or 17.2 miles out and back

Riding time: About 2.5 to 3 hours

Physical difficulty: Strenuous. The slickrock bed that underlies this route is severely tilted, causing extreme physical strain for Homo veloterra specimens who attempt to reach the formation's rim. Translation: This ride to the sky is steep.

Technical difficulty: Challenging. The ride starts out technically serene (moderate) and gets increasingly more challenging as it ascends the aforementioned slope. Want more challenge? Tack on the Portal Trail. Insane!

Trail surface: 4.7 miles on gravel road; 7.5 miles on four-wheel-drive road. This bad boy starts off on a packed dirt road, heads through some eroded spots, then finishes off with killer slickrock. It is a four-wheel-drive road in name only. The scrapes and an occasional grease stain are the only differences between a normal rock trail and the "jeep" route.

Land status: BLM

Maps: USGS Merrimac Butte, Gold Bar Rim, Moab

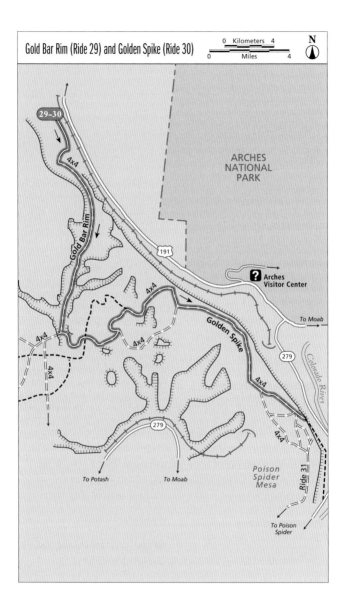

Gold Bar Rim (Ride 29) and Golden Spike (Ride 30)

0   Kilometers   4

0   Miles   4

N

29-30

4x4

Gold Bar Rim

191

ARCHES NATIONAL PARK

4x4

Golden Spike

? Arches Visitor Center

To Moab

4x4

279

Colorado River

4x4

4x4

4x4

4x4

4x4

279

To Potash

To Moab

Poison Spider Mesa

Ride 31

To Poison Spider

Finding the trailhead: From Center and Main Streets in Moab, head north 9.8 miles on US 191 and turn right. Follow the gravel road right and then left into the parking area. Ride the Moab Canyon Pathway to go under US 191 and start at the endpoint trailhead of Gemini Bridges Road (GPS: N38 39.111' / W109 40.099').

The Ride

0.0 After crossing under US 191 to the Gemini Bridges Road parking area, continue to head away from the highway, across the railroad tracks, and immediately left onto the gravel road. It's intermittently washboarded and eroded.

2.8 Stay on the main road up the hill and past the spurs. The road descends and levels out through a wide, rock-walled canyon.

4.6 Keep left at this wide-open intersection. Right heads up to Gemini Bridges.

4.8 After a quick entry into a canyon, the entrance to the Gold Bar Rim trail appears. Head left up the ledgy, scarred slickrock. The singletrack will start soon.

4.9 Look for the singletrack to the left. Follow the yellow dots.

6.0 A fork in the road. Keep left. Right will rejoin in 0.5 mile.

6.9 *Stay straight. The blue dot trail to the left is closed.* A ranger will bust you. They see everything.

7.1 The singletrack rejoins the four-by-four route. Left heads down the main four-by-four trail and right heads up it to the rim. You've come this far. It's just a bit farther (you'll hate me for saying that).

8.5 That closed trail rejoins from the left. Ignore it. It shouldn't be there. Move along.

8.6 You've reached the Golden Spike Trail. But you still want to see the view. Left goes up to the viewpoint. Go ahead—you've earned it.

This point delivers vistas of the La Sal Mountains ahead and the twisted terrain of Bull Canyon and Day Canyon behind.

Now it's time to put your exit strategy into motion. Returning the way you came or via the part of the four-by-four trail you skipped with the singletrack sounds good to your legs. Of course, you are at the junction of the next trail in the Mag-7. If you didn't plan ahead for it . . . *go back*.

17.2 It looks like you found your way back.

30 **Golden Spike**

OK, if you've made it this far and are willing to go farther, you're either in great shape, having an out-of-body experience and didn't know you could turn around, have a ton of water and food and supplies for an extended stay . . . or you're totally lost. Going farther without good biking fitness, plenty of water, and some trail food isn't very wise. So, you're up for this, right? OK. Golden Spike is the fifth trail in the Magnificent 7. The Golden Spike isn't that hard to follow. Besides the "sign" left behind by four-by-fours (Jeep scat), the route is marked with painted spots. It used to be marked with little painted spikes. The new markings are easier to follow.

Location: Way up high along the Gold Bar Rim

Distance: 5.4 miles point to point to the Portal Trail, 9.3 miles all the way to the road

Riding time: 2 hours

Physical difficulty: Extremely strenuous. It really is amazing how much climbing you can do without gaining any altitude. Simply amazing. Hey, it's something to think about other than the endless climbing you seem to be doing.

Technical difficulty: Challenging. You're over the technical stuff . . . you're too tired to care.

Trail surface: Hard, cracked, and bumpy. Halfway through this you may not even be aware that you have tires anymore as you suck the desert air into your lunch hoping an alien ship will come get you out of this wonderful little jaunt.

Land status: BLM

Maps: USGS Gold Bar Canyon

Finding the trailhead: You have to ride the Gold Bar Rim trail (Ride 29, GPS: N38 36.851' / W109 38.517') or the Poison Spider Mesa Trail (Ride 31, GPS: N38 34.583' / W109 36.330') to get here.

(See map with Ride 29.)

The Ride

0.0 Away you go from the junction with Gold Bar Rim trail. GPS: N38 36.851' / W109 38.517'.

0.8 Pass the Body Snatcher, Golden Stairs, and the Buggy Challenge— all names for things that are tough for four-by-fours. Next up is the Golden Crack.

0.9 A junction. Keep left even though the downhill to the right looks kinder to your legs. Say, did you notice the huge hole coming up on your right? That's called the Golden Crack. Look, I know you're tired, but no jokes about the landmark names, OK? GPS: N38 36.515' / W109 38.134'.

1.1 Climbed back up . . . again. GPS: N38 36.610' / W109 37.945'.

1.3 Yup, the world is still there. GPS: N38 36.529' / W109 37.559'.

1.8 Is the entrance to Arches National Park over there? GPS: N38 36.333' / W109 37.048'.

1.9 Yup, that's Arches over there. But we're turning back down again. GPS: N38 36.247' / W109 36.931'.

3.2 Really? Oh goodie, back up we go! GPS: N38 35.839' / W109 36.722'.

3.7 Probably a good idea to turn right here instead of pedaling off the cliff. GPS: N38 35.916' / W109 36.550'.

4.6 Does this ever end? N38 35.026' / W109 36.300'.

5.4 That was a cool section. Like a cave with a sunroof. After some nice slickrock—even though you did have to climb some of it—you've been deposited on red sand. This is important. Turn to your left for a Portal Trail exit. If you keep going straight, you'll be exiting via Poison Spider. Technically you're now on the Poison Spider Trail. GPS: N38 34.583' / W109 36.330'.

6.8 No . . . really? The Portal. GPS: N38 35.030' / W109 35.686'.

7.8   Slow for the skinny spot that everyone talks about. There may even be a sign warning you of impending doom. If you have any doubt, carry your bike over this rock. The move itself wouldn't be too bad if it weren't for the 200-foot bunny hop on the outside. Even the best full suspension won't soften that landing. Funny thing is, the hard part of the trail follows.

9.0   Read the comments in the trail registration box here. This is where everybody tries to think of a creative way to say that the Portal Trail was really neat.

9.3   The trail ends at Potash Road. You finished that? You animal! Do you even own a car? Why? If you're still conscious, don't wander into traffic. Surely you planned on how to get back . . . and eat.

31 **Poison Spider Mesa and the Portal Trail**

This famous must-do trail is a technical, physical, and mental workout. Views of the Behind the Rocks fins set against the La Sals are an obvious photo op, as is Little Arch. The slickrock is massive, the sand annoying, and the Portal is downright dangerous. Its narrowest portion is about 3 feet wide with a 400-foot drop on the left and a rock wall on the right. A technically challenging boulder hop on the skinniest part is avoidable by riding a 4-inch-wide patch of dirt directly on the cliff edge. It's probably wise to carry your bike past the exposed part. Unfortunately, the most technically difficult part of the Portal comes later. While not exposed, it is still technically challenging all the way down. It is also walkable, but it's not a pleasant stroll and can cause trouble for those still on their steeds. Walking the narrowest point of the Portal Trail is strongly advised. The trail is very popular with bikes, four-by-fours, and ATVs. If there is a four-by-four event in town, you may want to get your Poison Spider experience in town. Oh yeah, the trail is marked with small images of Jeeps on the slickrock.

Location: 10 miles west of Moab

Distance: 12.9-mile loop via the Portal Trail or 12.8 miles out and back

Riding time: About 2 to 4 hours

Physical difficulty: Strenuous. The initial climb starts the muscle burn, the sand sucks any reserves, and the slickrock steeps finish the job. The upper body gets a workout with the technical sections, especially on the Portal Trail.

Technical difficulty: Challenging. Within its first 0.5 mile, the road turns technical with a loose-rock climb. Later, slickrock staircases pose extreme

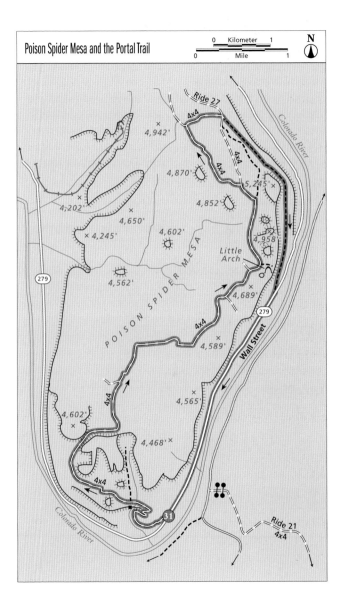

Poison Spider Mesa and the Portal Trail

0 Kilometer 1
0 Mile 1

N

Ride 27

4x4

4,942'

4,870'

4x4

4x4

5,245'

4,852'

4,202'

x

4,650'

4,958'

x 4,245'

4,602'

Little Arch

4,562'

P O I S O N   S P I D E R   M E S A

4,689'

279

Wall Street

4x4

4,589'

4x4

4,565'

4,602'

x

4,468' x

4x4

31

Colorado River

Colorado River

Ride 21

4x4

Colorado River

tests of ledging abilities. Sand and slickrock steeps complete the recipe for a classic ride. The icing on the cake is the Portal Trail, which is a technical and mental challenge. Some difficult moves occur where there is no room for error. Fall here, and you won't land for another 400 feet. *Cyclists have died here*.

Trail surface: While listed as four-wheel-drive road, a majority of this ride is anything but a road. When on slickrock it follows blazes painted on the rock. The Portal Trail loop option includes 2.5 miles of singletrack. This ride has a classic recipe: Start with packed dirt. Add some ruts, loose rocks, sand, bedrock ledges, and slickrock. Mix well. For easier riding, let soak in a good rain. For a looser, more difficult ride, do not add liquids. Use only premium-grade Moab slickrock.

Land status: BLM

Maps: USGS Moab, Gold Bar Rim

Finding the trailhead: From Center and Main Streets in Moab, drive 4.3 miles north on US 191 to Potash Road, UT 279. Travel west past the ruins, the Portal Trail's terminus, "Wall Street," and the petroglyphs to the "Dinosaur Tracks" sign at mile 10.4 that marks the trailhead. Go 0.1 mile up the dirt road to a parking area. The trailhead has a pit toilet and an information kiosk. GPS: N38 31.945' / W109 36.549'

The Ride

0.0   Potash Road. Head up the gravel road. A BLM information display and parking are at the 0.1-mile mark. Most people will actually start riding at the 0.1-mile mark.

0.4   The road forks; stay right.

0.5   This technical spot is just an itty-bitty sample of what lies ahead.

0.9   This loose and steep hill looks much easier than it is . . . and it doesn't look that easy.

1.0 The road turns right and goes down briefly in a technically moderate-to-challenging move (but rank it challenging on the way back).

1.3 The road bends to the left and remains eroded and moderately technical.

1.4 Stay right past the faint spur here.

1.6 Another spur goes left; stay right.

2.1 The action gets fast and furious after the sand makes its entrance. Just ahead lie some brutal climbing, slickrock, more sand, and then some ledges for a barrage of moderate-to-challenging obstacles.

2.4 Mac-Daddy sand trap.

2.5 Go up this technically challenging patch of rock, then right at the fork to follow the painted white "Jeeps" stenciled on the rock.

2.9 More sand, then more slickrock and a view of Behind the Rocks.

3.1 After this slickrock steep, go left at the fork following the painted diamond (the Jeeps go right).

3.5 The trails rejoin and bear left.

3.6 Keep left at this slickrock transition for the easier (moderate-to-challenging) way up. Right is a technically challenging move.

3.9 Stay left here.

5.8 Ugh. Another monster sand trap.

6.0 The road forks; stay right.

6.4 After a slickrock ascent, park the bikes, and head off to the right to see Little Arch. This is the spot where you'll turn around if you're not riding the Portal Trail.

6.5 Back on the trail. The slickrock becomes a steep up-and-down roller coaster.

6.7 The track forks; stay left.

7.2 Go left up the slickrock wall. Then head for a low notch in the rock formations. Cairns and jeeps may point the way, but don't count on it. Simply head to the rock wall and look for the notch through it. To the right is a sandy, hard-to-follow trail that eventually leads to the Portal. Left makes more sense.

7.7 The road becomes visible again, then forks. Turn right and head back up the hill. It gets ledgy as it climbs to the rim.

8.3 Top. The Portal Trail goes right. Views here extend into Moab, the Slickrock Trail, Arches National Park, and the La Sals. This becomes a gathering area in busy times, like a ski area. Riders size up each other before heading down the Portal Trail. GPS: N38 35.031' / W109 35.683'.

9.3 Slow for the skinny spot that everyone talks about. If you have any doubts (sense?), carry your bike over this rock. The move itself wouldn't be too bad if it weren't for the 400-foot bunny hop on the

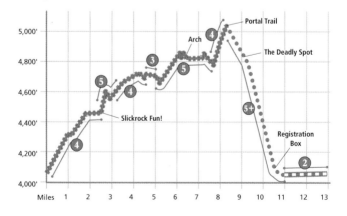

outside. Even the best full suspension won't soften that landing. The hard part follows.

10.5 Read the comments in the trail registration box here. This is where everybody tries to think of a creative way to say that the Portal Trail was really neat.

10.8 The trail ends at the Potash Road. Turn right to return to the car. Beware of the big trucks that roar down the road. They, too, have claimed a biker's life.

12.9 Turn right and climb up to the parking lot.

32 Intrepid Trail System at Dead Horse Point

Dead Horse Point has always been a place to visit on any trip to Moab. It is steeped in Old West history and has stunning views of Canyon Country. It's an amazing place. The problem for many bikers was justifying the trip into the park. There wasn't anywhere to ride. That's been remedied with eight interconnected, singletrack loops: Intrepid, Great Pyramid, Big Chief, Raven Roll, Crossroads, Whiptail, Twisted Tree, and Prickly Pair. A quick lap with Intrepid, Great Pyramid, and Raven Roll will provide a good sample of this area. No dogs allowed on any of these trails.

Location: 32.5 miles north and west of Moab

Distance: From 1.1 miles to 9.0 miles. Of course, these are loops so you can increase distances if you so choose.

Riding time: About 1 to 3 hours. Don't forget to plan time to sit and absorb the surroundings at the viewpoints. Got lunch?

Physical difficulty: The area's trails run the gamut from easy to moderately strenuous.

Technical difficulty: Moderate. Intrepid Loop is moderately easy.

Trail surface: Singletrack and slickrock

Land status: Dead Horse Point State Park (435-259-2614)

Maps: USGS Gold Bar Canyon. The trail junctions are well signed. Ask for a free map at the ranger station and bring it along. It sheds light on the nature around you.

Finding the trailhead: From Center and Main Streets in Moab, take US 191 north 11 miles. Turn left onto UT 313. Bear left 14.6 miles past US 191, following UT 313 and the signs to Dead Horse Point State Park. Continue

Intrepid Trail System at Dead Horse Point

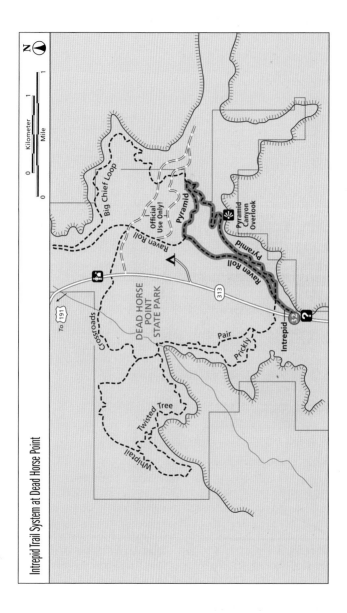

6.5 miles to the trailhead. The trail leaves the northern end of the parking lot. GPS: N38 31.945' / W109 36.549'

- -

Intrepid Trail

This is the easiest trail here. It doesn't climb much and is very short. The problem is that many true beginners will find the broken terrain difficult to ascend. Seasoned riders might not even notice and may wonder why their dates are struggling. The grade is so gentle that many new riders never feel the need to shift into lower gears. Easier gears make it easier to keep your wheels rolling across any rocks or roots that get in your way, thus keeping your momentum. This is a good thing.

Distance: 1.1 miles point to point
Physical difficulty: Easy
Technical difficulty: Moderately easy
Trail surface: Slickrock slabs and dirt singletrack
Navigation tips: The start is a shared section of trail. You may have to wait for a group going the other way. Make sure you don't ride on the "hiking only" trail that parallels the start. When a true beginner or child decides they've had enough, they are probably almost to the Colorado Overlook. You can make it! Walking your bike is a perfectly acceptable way to continue.

- -

Pyramid Loop

This is a good place to start for most. The first 0.4 mile is along the Intrepid Trail. Afterward, the technical challenges increase. The goal here is to get to the Pyramid Canyon Overlook. After a suitable amount of gawking, the ride continues. Some technical climbing on tight, rocky, and sandy switchbacks will be the hardest things ahead. That and the fact that you'll be gaining some altitude.

Distance: 3.9-mile loop
Physical difficulty: Moderate

Technical difficulty: Moderate. Some rocky ledges and tight turns will test your skills.

Trail surface: Slickrock, singletrack, and some sand
Navigation tips: The turn to continue on Great Pyramid is well signed. Miss it and you'll be doing twice as much riding. If you have beginners, you can ride with them to the Colorado River Overlook before abandoning them as you continue your journey (GPS: N 38 29.619' / W 109 43.765').

Big Chief Loop

Distance: 9.0-mile loop
Physical difficulty: Moderately strenuous
Technical difficulty: Moderate
Trail surface: Singletrack, slickrock, and some sand
Navigation tips: If you have beginners, you can ride with them to the Colorado River Overlook before abandoning them as you continue your journey. If you have less-fit members in your group, you can ride with them to the Pyramid Canyon Overlook before deserting them as you continue your quest (GPS: N 38 30.243' / W 109 42.880').

Raven Roll

A rolling road through the desert grasses.

Distance: 1.6 miles point to point
Physical difficulty: Easy
Technical difficulty: Easily moderate
Trail surface: Smooth, dirt doubletrack
Navigation tips: The trail links Big Chief, Pyramid, and Intrepid together and joins with Crossroads to link the western trails as well. It can get soft in spots (GPS: N 38 30.704' / W 109 43.294').

Crossroads

What starts as a basic connector east of the highway turns into a pleasant jaunt in the desert piñon.

Distance: 1.7 miles point to point
Physical difficulty: Moderately easy
Technical difficulty: Moderately easy

Trail surface: Smooth, singletrack with some soft sand
Navigation tips: Be aware of your abilities before riding Whiptail, Twisted Tree, and Prickly Pair, which connect to this trail. Those are all more difficult (GPS: N 38 30.704' / W 109 43.294').

Whiptail

Get into the rhythm of this trail's flow but don't forget to enjoy the views.

Distance: 2.6 miles point to point
Physical difficulty: Moderate
Technical difficulty: Moderate
Trail surface: Flowy singletrack

Navigation tips: Whiptail joins with Crossroads, Twisted Tree, and Prickly Pair (GPS: N 38 30.638' / W 109 44.548').

Twisted Tree

The views here make up for a couple of sandy patches and challenging climbs. Good stuff!

Distance: 1.5 miles point to point
Physical difficulty: Moderate
Technical difficulty: Moderately challenging
Trail surface: Flowing singletrack with some sand traps

Navigation tips: It's still mostly smooth sailing that connects to Prickly Pair and Whiptail (GPS: N 38 30.607' / W 109 45.441').

Prickly Pair

Distance: 2.2 miles point to point (1.8 via Pair)
Physical difficulty: Moderate
Technical difficulty: Moderately challenging
Trail surface: Smooth, dirt doubletrack

Navigation tips: Actually 2 trails. Prickly is the main trail while Pair is a tad shorter and easier. Connects to Twisted Tree (GPS: N 38 29.578' / W 109 43.980').

The Ride

0.0   Leave the parking area on the north side. Be careful as the trail has traffic of all abilities going in both directions. Don't worry, things will thin out. The tread is ever-so-slightly ledgy here and many beginners might have trouble as they learn how to deal with it.

0.3   Prickly Pair, technically rated as moderate-to-challenging, leaves to the left. Raven Roll enters dead ahead. Bear right on Intrepid Trail.

0.4   Keep right at this junction with Raven Roll. The trail changes its name here to Great Pyramid.

2.0   Turn left to complete Pyramid. Straight ahead is the much longer Big Chief trail.

2.6   Turn left onto Raven Roll.

3.5   Back at the junction with Intrepid and Pyramid. If you've had enough, the parking lot is just ahead. Otherwise, check out the map and do another lap.

3.9   Parking lot.

33 **Jug Handle Loop—The Shafer Trail**

Making it to the top of the Shafer Trail is a rush for hammerheads, and the descent down Long Canyon will thrill downhillers. The trail climbs gradually through a dramatic, desolate landscape wrought with crumbling cliffs. At the White Rim the climb becomes a brutal slap in the face. Long Canyon features Pucker Pass, which requires a heads-up move on rough terrain before diving into the depths of the canyon below. Make sure your brakes are in top shape!

Location: 18 miles west of Moab

Distance: 36.5-mile loop

Riding time: About 3 to 6 hours

Physical difficulty: Strenuous. The climb up the Shafer Trail is major-league. It rises 1,240 feet in 3 miles, gaining 920 feet of that from miles 17 to 18.5.

Technical difficulty: Moderate. Most of this ride is free of major technical sections. But the drop through Pucker Pass in Long Canyon has some solid moderate-to-challenging riding and tight switchbacks that come up faster than lunch on a roller coaster.

Trail surface: 25.7 miles on gravel and four-wheel-drive roads; 10.8 miles on paved road. The gravel and four-wheel-drive roads are basically packed clay. When wet it's slicker than snot on a glass doorknob and is best avoided. The upper portion of Long Canyon is rocky and eroded. The pavement is comparatively smooth, hard, and black, with white and yellow paint occurring in definite patterns.

Land status: BLM and Canyonlands National Park

Maps: USGS Shafer Basin, Musselman Arch, The Knoll

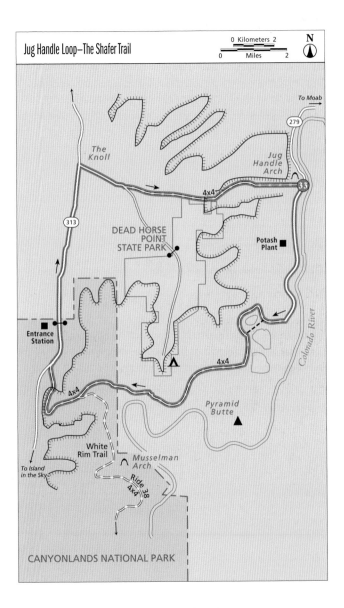

Jug Handle Loop—The Shafer Trail

0 Kilometers 2
0 Miles 2

N

To Moab

279

The Knoll

Jug Handle Arch

4x4

33

313

DEAD HORSE POINT STATE PARK

Potash Plant

Entrance Station

Colorado River

4x4

4x4

Pyramid Butte

To Island in the Sky

White Rim Trail

Musselman Arch

Ride 38 4x4

CANYONLANDS NATIONAL PARK

Finding the trailhead: From the visitor center in downtown Moab, drive 4.3 miles north on US 191. Turn left onto UT 279 (Potash Road) and drive another 14.1 miles to a trailhead parking area immediately after the Jug Handle Arch on the right, across a set of railroad tracks. Both the arch and the parking area are signed. Potash Road also has signed archaeological and dinosaur points of interest en route to the parking area (GPS: N 38 32.789' / W 109 38.878').

The Ride

0.0 From the parking area, turn right onto Potash Road and pedal south along the Colorado River.

1.7 Intersection. Go straight and pass the potash plant.

3.1 The road turns to dirt then begins to climb.

4.1 Top this hill and enjoy a brief downhill run, then grind up and over another rise.

5.2 Getting "board"—washboard, that is!

5.5 Currently the route goes straight through a four-way intersection. Obey the signs! The potash plant managers reroute traffic depending upon their evaporative needs.

9.2 A spur heads left to a Colorado River overlook. Pyramid Butte is now to stern.

9.9 Keep on the main road here. The first spur right beats itself against the canyon wall. Another faint spur dead-ends to the left.

11.8 Keep right on the main road as it makes a sweeping 90-degree turn.

14.4 Through the wash and up. The going gets a bit technical ahead as the road weaves up the south fork of Shafer Canyon.

15.1 Relief is in sight (it's usually well supplied with toilet paper).

16.1 Turn right at the intersection in Shafer Camp and enjoy the initial gradual climb. Left heads off to Musselman Arch on the White Rim Trail.

17.0 From this point most people awaken to what's ahead of them. Think motivational thoughts. Does it help to know that the climb tapers off in 1.9 miles after gaining 1,000 feet?

18.9 Yes, but it helps even more to know that a 1,000-foot elevation gain is behind you. Look off to the right to see the spaghetti-like road below. This is called the Neck. The bend in the Colorado is labeled Goose Neck.

21.4 After a much more mellow climb, the road meets the Island in the Sky Road inside Canyonlands National Park. Turn right and head out on this paved road.

27.3 Turn right toward Dead Horse Point on UT 313.

28.9 Bear left onto the dirt road as UT 313 veers right. The road is marked with a stop sign. Remain on this road, passing numerous spurs as it rolls through juniper highlands.

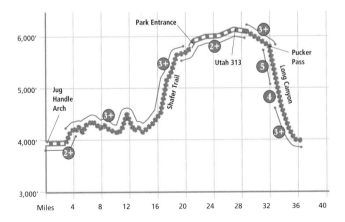

29.9 Stay right and rattle over washboards.

32.1 The road bends left and down, giving a view of Poison Spider Mesa, Behind the Rocks, and the La Sals before diving through Pucker Pass into Long Canyon.

35.5 Time to flex the hands. A mach-5 downhill tapers off for a relaxing finish to the car.

36.5 Arrive back at the trailhead.

34 Hey Joe Green Loop

This nice rolling road suddenly sprouts teeth as it rocks down into Spring Canyon in search of the river. The road is sandy but firm as it follows the Green River's twists between steep canyon walls. The route ducks in and out of gauntlets of tamarisk trees. The zombie-stepping, one-hand-free portage is a climb with some exposure that requires shoes with good soles. From the top it's a long, gradually ascending ride home.

Location: 26 miles northeast of Moab

Distance: 33.4-mile loop plus a steep, technical 0.5-mile portage

Riding time: About 4 to 6 hours

Physical difficulty: Moderately strenuous. The hills are fairly gradual but slow-going. Sand, distance, and the portage add up to a physically draining ride.

Technical difficulty: Moderate. While the majority of the ride is in the moderate range, dropping into Spring Canyon is tricky and unforgiving, a moderate-to-challenging pitch. Keep momentum in the sand traps along the Green River. The portage is tough; it climbs steeply up slickrock and broken bedrock with a small degree of exposure.

Trail surface: 16.6 miles on gravel road; 16.8 miles on four-wheel-drive road; 0.5-mile portage. The gravel road has a few mild washboard sections. The four-wheel-drive descent into Spring Canyon is rocky, and the riverside is soft but rideable sand.

Land status: BLM

Maps: USGS Dubinky, Bow Knot, Tenmile Point

Finding the trailhead: Set your car's trip odometer to 0.0 at Center Street in Moab and drive 11 miles north on US 191. Turn left onto UT 313 and follow signs toward Dead Horse Point and Canyonlands. At mile 19.5 (8.5 miles from US 191), turn right onto Dubinky Well Road. This dirt road leaves UT 313 after a gradual left-hand bend. Stay on this main road,

Hey Joe Green Loop

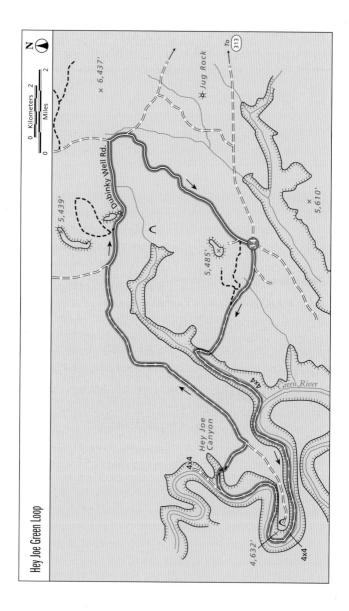

keeping left at the prominent spur at mile 21 that goes to Dubinky Well. Again, stay on the main road passing any spurs. Roll up to a four-way intersection at the top of a hill at mile 25.9. This is the trailhead. GPS: N38 37.626' / W109 55.668'

The Ride

0.0 From the four-way intersection, continue in the original direction of travel, away from UT 313. Remain on this road, avoiding all spurs.

3.4 This wash has a nasty drop. The road skirts the cliff side, then begins a wild, technical downhill.

4.6 The descent ends in this wash. Climb out to the right onto the road. Don't forget to look up at the canyon walls as you press on.

6.2 The road forks; keep right and begin heading upriver.

6.7 The big, rusty object on the right is an old ferry mooring.

7.4 The doubletrack is sandy and overgrown.

9.2 A technically moderate-to-challenging patch.

11.8 Race along the riverbank, then into tamarisk hollows.

14.3 An old bulldozer marks a right-hand turn up into twisted Hey Joe Canyon and conjures images of Ed Abbey's Monkey Wrench Gang.

15.1 This climb gets rough, then skirts the Hey Joe Mine. Continue past the mine, then look for a trail to switchback farther up the canyon and above the mine. The best of the numerous trails here heads upcanyon a way before switching back to scramble up the bench. Rig up (shoulder your bike) and follow the cairns. This hair-raising portage twists up slickrock and broken rock and requires a free hand for balance. Falling here ain't healthy. A few spots ease off enough to be rideable, but this never lasts long.

15.5 A rusted gas tank marks the finish of the portage. This odometer reading is a good restarting point. The road ahead is flat and often sandy.

15.7 Turn left at a T intersection. Right heads to an arch.

16.7 Another T intersection; go left. A few spurs leave this road, but you stay on the main road. A rugged climb awaits before giving way to a gradual spin.

23.6 A road joins from the left, followed shortly by a gate. Please close the gate behind you.

25.2 The rock formation that looks like a person on his back with a foot stone is called the Needles. The next right-hand spur heads 1.7 miles to a tubelike arch formation.

27.2 Turn right onto the gravel road. To the left the road heads to Dubinky Well and then to Blue Hills Road. But right leads home.

27.7 The road forks; turn right for a gradual ascent to the trailhead. Dubinky Road continues left to rejoin the access road before UT 313.

32.5 Turn left at a T intersection.

33.4 End the loop back at your car.

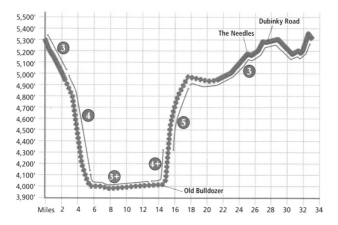

35 **Boxcar Bridge**

Beginning with a gradual spin, the ride turns technical as it dives into the isolated head of Trout Water Canyon. Boxcar Bridge comes into view high on a hill, then the trail turns into a cottonwood–lined wash near an old homestead. Sand traps force most riders to push in a couple of spots, but such desert solitude is worth it. Other people are rarely seen on this route.

Location: 50 miles south of Moab in the Canyon Rims Recreational Area

Distance: 21.4-mile loop

Riding time: About 2.5 to 4 hours

Physical difficulty: Moderately strenuous. Most of the ride has a gradual grade, but a couple of climbs are strenuous (and sandy too).

Technical difficulty: Moderate. Some eroded sections are moderate to challenging, but the majority of the ride is on mild, rustic road.

Trail surface: 7.3 miles on gravel; 14.1 miles on four-wheel-drive roads that begin as packed dirt, then become sandy and eroded in the canyon

Land status: Canyon Rims Recreational District

Map: USGS Eightmile Rock

Finding the trailhead: From Center and Main Streets in Moab, drive 34.2 miles south on US 191 to the Canyon Rims Recreational Area. Turn right onto CR 133, also known as Needles Overlook Road. Follow this paved road 15.1 miles west to a Y junction. Take the right-hand fork (Anticline Road) and drive 0.7 mile north. Turn right onto Eightmile Rock Road (CR 132) and park. GPS: N38 16.066' / W109 34.390'

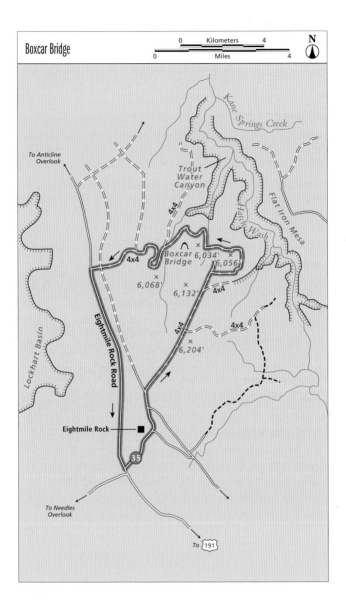

Boxcar Bridge

Kilometers
0   4
0   Miles   4

N

To Anticline
Overlook

Kane Springs Creek

Trout
Water
Canyon

Hatch Wash

Flat Iron Mesa

4x4

4x4

Boxcar 6,034'
Bridge ×
× 6,056'

× 6,068'

× 6,132'

4x4

4x4

4x4

× 6,204'

4x4

Lockhart Basin

Eightmile Rock Road

Eightmile Rock ■

35

To Needles
Overlook

To 191

The Ride

0.0 Head up Eightmile Rock Road.

1.1 Briefly descend to a fork and go left, past the old structures built into the rock.

1.6 Keep right here, heeding the "Danger" sign.

2.0 Bear left onto a gravel road.

2.2 Cross a bright-yellow cattle guard.

2.3 Turn right onto an arrow-straight road through the brush. The ride remains on this main road for a few miles.

3.9 Pass by the cattle trough, ignoring spur roads.

4.2 A spur goes right; keep left.

4.4 A spur goes left; keep right.

4.7 Crest a small rise. Junipers dot the landscape.

5.2 The road forks; go left. The road becomes rougher and increasingly overgrown.

5.9 A faint road—more like overgrown doubletrack—leaves to the right, and you'll follow it to complete the loop. But first go straight for 0.25 mile to a viewpoint well worth the extra distance.

6.2 Top the hill and roll to the viewpoint. Trout Water Canyon lies ahead, with rippled slickrock below, while the ever-present La Sals frame the horizon. Backtrack to the road mentioned at mile 5.9.

6.4 Back at the 5.9-mile spot. Take the fork less traveled, which is now a left turn.

6.7 The doubletrack becomes patchy rock, gravel, and sand on an eroded descent through rock outcroppings and old-growth junipers.

7.3 The road turns left up a sandy hill followed by a soft, sandy descent. This is a fun surf!

8.4 The tread is heavily eroded after this turn. Watch the ruts! Cross a sandy wash and claw up a brutally sandy hill. Ride the erosion ruts for any chance of reaching the top without pushing. Ignore the numerous cow paths braiding off the main track.

8.9 Top the hill only to tackle another, more rideable hill. The upcoming descent is gradual on a sand and grass doubletrack.

9.3 The road bears left. Don't be fooled by the cow paths.

9.7 Hang on for a rough and rutted descent, with some smooth spots tossed in for good measure. Wheee!

10.1 Bounce through a sand and slickrock wash, then scramble up a loose, rock-strewn climb.

10.4 Look north for the view over Trout Water Canyon to Prostitute Butte and the Behind the Rocks region.

10.9 Boxcar Bridge can easily be seen high up on the butte ahead and to the left.

11.4 Cross another wash.

11.8 Ugh . . . another loose, eroded, rocky climb. Rate it at moderate to challenging.

12.2 Keep right on the doubletrack as a cow trail heads left.

12.4 Grab the brakes for an eroded descent with a technically challenging spot at mile 12.5.

12.6 T into a sandy doubletrack and turn left. Cross the wash. Right is the return portion of the Trout Water Canyon Trail (see appendix B: Additional Rides).

12.9 The road is still sandy as it goes into a wash. Follow the wash to the left for 100 yards and then exit on the right-hand side.

13.2 Into the wash again, then out the left side toward the huge cottonwoods. Pass through the gate in the grove.

13.4 Wobble up the gullied road to a switchback fork. Stay right and up. Left leads to Trout Water Spring. The road becomes less sandy, but small sand traps (baby bunkers?) still lurk.

14.2 A not-so-neonatal sand trap.

14.4 Bear right on the slickrock to pick up the trail.

14.6 Grunt up a soft climb.

14.9 Top. Stay left as a road joins from the right (the final leg of the Trout Water Canyon loop).

15.4 The tread improves. Keep right at a Y junction and stay on the main road from here to Anticline Road.

16.3 Anticline Road. Stop to enjoy the view through Lockhart Canyon and beyond. Then look for traffic and turn left, pedaling south on rolling gravel road.

21.4 Loop is complete. Where's a tall glass of lemonade when you need one?

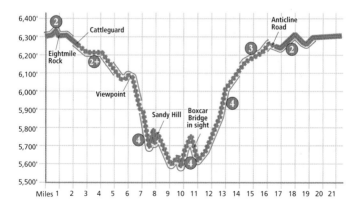

36 **Colorado River Overlook**

Gazing down on the Colorado River after pumping through the desert puts things into perspective—life is good. This is a great way to experience this section of Canyonlands without all the technical and aerobic difficulties of the Confluence Trail. It's a good first ride from the nearby campground.

Location: 70 miles south of Moab in Canyonlands National Park

Distance: 14.6 miles out and back

Riding time: About 2 to 3 hours

Physical difficulty: Moderate. The road grade is pretty gradual; the main energy drains come in small doses. Save some water for the final 2.5-mile climb on the return trip.

Technical difficulty: Moderate. This makes a good first ride in the

Needles District to gauge skills. Hazards—mainly eroded ruts and potholes—are well exposed.

Trail surface: 14.6 miles on four-wheel-drive road. The road is mainly packed dirt with some exposed rock and occasional eroded patches.

Land status: Canyonlands National Park, Needles District

Map: USGS The Loop

Finding the trailhead: From Center Street in Moab, drive 42.6 miles south on US 191 to the well-signed junction with UT 211 and turn right. Stay on this paved road for 38 miles, all the way to the entrance gate, and pay the fee. Park at the visitor center, which is also the trailhead. GPS: N38 10.135' / W109 45.630'. Allow time on the drive to visit Newspaper Rock. This pullout on the road into Canyonlands is a primo rock art site. The entrance fee is $10 per vehicle. Receipts are good for four days, and an annual pass is $50. Entrance fees to Canyonlands are good in all districts.

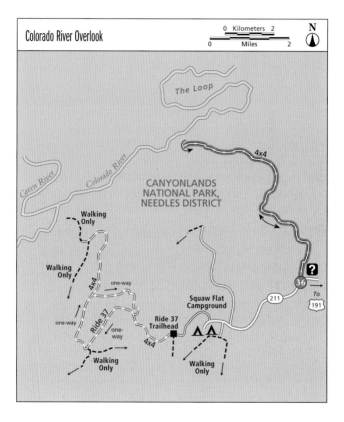

Colorado River Overlook

0 Kilometers 2
0 Miles 2

N

The Loop

4x4

Green River

Colorado River

CANYONLANDS
NATIONAL PARK,
NEEDLES DISTRICT

Walking
Only

Walking
Only

4x4

one-way

Walking
Only

one-way

Ride 37

one-way

Squaw Flat
Campground

Ride 37
Trailhead

4x4

?

36

211

To
191

Walking
Only

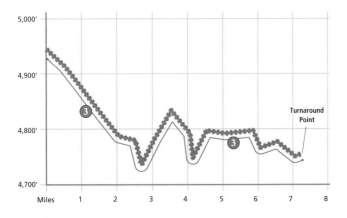

The Ride

0.0   The four-wheel-drive trail leaves the north (left) side of the parking lot. The track immediately forks—follow the sign pointing left. The first 2 miles descend gradually into the head of Salt Creek.

2.7   Another fork; keep right. The left-hand trail leads to the Lower Jump and is definitely worth the 0.15-mile hike (no bikes, please) down. The main route begins a moderate climb north out of the Salt Creek drainage, then rolls west toward the Colorado.

7.3   Trail's end. Look down about 1,000 feet to see the waters of the Colorado River rolling out of an enormous oxbow known as the Loop. From here the river flows about 4 miles to the confluence with the Green River.

14.6   Arrive back at the trailhead.

37 **Confluence Overlook**

OK, so it sounds tiring and tough. It is. But the payoff—a short hike to see the confluence of the Green and Color-Red-Oh! Rivers—is worth the effort. When the rivers run true to their names, the mixing of color is spectacular. Bring a lock to secure your bike while hiking. Also use chain lube that sets up dry to minimize sand damage. And bring some cash for the park entrance fee.

Location: 70 miles south of Moab in Canyonlands National Park

Distance: 15.3-mile lariat-shaped loop

Riding time: About 3 to 5 hours plus at least an hour for the hike and gaping

Physical difficulty: Strenuous. The initial climb saps your strength, then the sand finishes you off.

Technical difficulty: Moderate to challenging. Once ridden, Elephant Hill is never forgotten. Good sand skills are a big plus for this journey.

Trail surface: 15.3 miles on four-wheel-drive road. It starts off with rock steps up Elephant Hill, then gets sandy heading down Devil's Lane.

Land status: Canyonlands National Park, Needles District

Map: USGS The Loop

Finding the trailhead: From Center Street in Moab, drive 42.6 miles south on US 191 to the well-signed junction with UT 211 and turn right. Go west 38 miles on this paved road all the way to the entrance gate and Needles District visitor center and pay the fee ($10/vehicle). From the visitor center, continue 2.7 miles west on UT 211 and turn left toward Squaw Flat Campground. Keep right twice to the gravel road to Elephant Hill. The trailhead parking area is 5.1 miles from the visitor center. GPS: N38 08.674' / W109 48.882'. Allow time on the drive in to visit Newspaper Rock. This rock art site along the road into Canyonlands will help set the mood for the ride ahead.

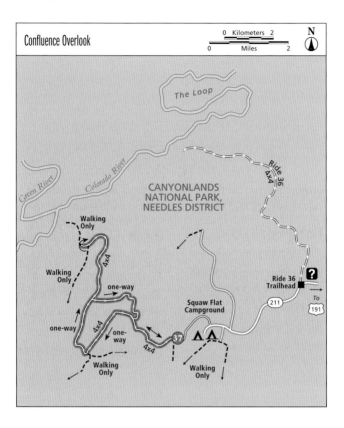

0 Kilometers 2

0 Miles 2

N

The Loop

Green River

Colorado River

CANYONLANDS
NATIONAL PARK,
NEEDLES DISTRICT

Ride 36
4x4

Walking
Only

4x4

Walking
Only

one-way

Ride 36
Trailhead

?

one-way

Squaw Flat
Campground

211

To
191

one-way

4x4

4x4

one-way

37

Walking
Only

Walking
Only

The Ride

0.0 Elephant Hill. You'll never forget the rock ledges and crags among the sand. It gets ya' comin' and goin'.

1.5 Turn left onto the one-way road (it's one-way for bikers too). The sounds you've been hearing are the gasps of disbelief as your brain tries to take in the surroundings.

2.0 After crossing the wash, bear left and head into Devil's Pocket.

3.4 Turn right away from the Devil's Kitchen campsite and down toward Devil's Lane.

4.0 Turn right onto Devil's Lane and follow it straight through sand hell. Sing along with the Steve Miller Band: "You've got to go through hell before you get to heaven."

5.4 Keep left and pass the one-way road home going right.

7.8 Keep right and whirl past Cyclone Canyon to the end of the road.

8.6 This parking area means it's time to dismount. Park rangers say it's OK to lock bikes to the hitching post or gently to a juniper. Cable locks work, but the Krypto-style won't. Hike 1 mile from here to the confluence overlook. The hike mileage is not included in the odometer readings. After enjoying the world of grandeur, walk back, remount, and begin the journey back to civilization.

9.4 Turn left, retracing the route past Cyclone Canyon.

11.8 Turn left on the one-way road (see mile 5.4 above).

13.8 Turn left and head back over Elephant Hill. Unless you want to do another lap.

15.3 This epic ride is complete.

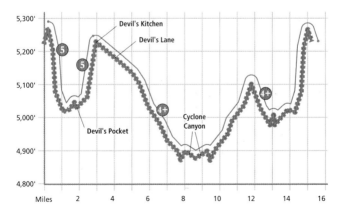

38 **White Rim**

The White Rim is famous as the ultimate Canyon Country ride. Though more and more people ride this in one day, they're missing the point. This trail is about being with friends in one of the most scenic regions in the world.

Do this ride clockwise with a four-wheel-drive sag vehicle. Aiming for Gooseberry, Murphy, and Hardscrabble Campgrounds makes for a good, moderate ride with one aerobic assault daily. Spring and fall are the prime times to make this epic journey. Don't even think of riding this during summer. It's just too hot and is probably unsafe. No-see-ums usually become a problem in late May and stick around into summer. Riding clockwise puts the Green River at the end of the trip, a possible emergency water source from Queen Anne's Bottom to Mineral Bottom (purify all water). If time and supplies allow, camp in the Island in the Sky Campground the night before the journey. Also be sure you're stocked up on water before leaving town. The park doesn't have any water for visitors. Plan on at least a gallon a day per rider plus water for creature comforts. Low-impact campers will be happy they learned about the dishwashing properties of sand.

Location: 30 miles west of Moab in the Island in the Sky District of Canyonlands National Park

Distance: 103.1-mile loop

Riding time: About 10 hours plus a nap and meals for the superhuman, or a 3- to 5-day sag-supported (four-wheel-drive

required) expedition for mortals. The ride described here goes clockwise around the loop in 4 days and 3 nights.

Physical difficulty: Moderate. To attempt this 103.1-mile loop as a day ride borders on psychotic. As a multi-day ride it ranks as moderate, with one major

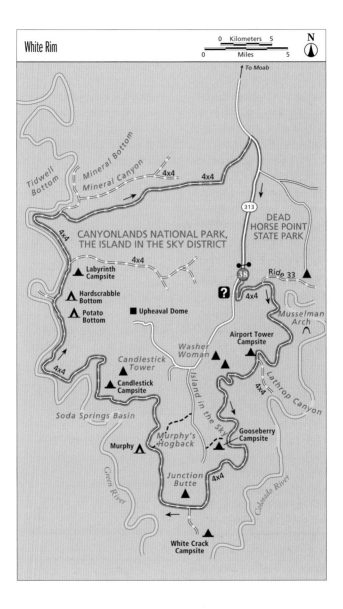

(strenuous!) climb scheduled for each day. Day 1 consists of a huge descent, then easy grades. Day 2 adds some climbing near White Crack and then a frightfully steep wall innocently named Murphy's Hogback. More descending starts day 3 for some great unwinding, but, to keep riders honest, Hardscrabble is a day's worth of climbing in one shot. The final day sees a long sandy spin along the Green River and an inhuman climb up Horsethief Trail. This is followed by a long gradual grind that is easily avoided with a shuttle.

Technical difficulty: Moderate. A few slickrock patches, bedrock drops, and eroded ruts keep things interesting. But these obstacles are small and widely spread out. The fast and furious drop down the Shafer Trail has savage grades and harrowing hairpins. The rest of the day's spin is mild, with some ledges near camp. The road to White Crack, on day 2, includes a steep, sandy hill that is very tough to clean. Murphy's Hogback is so steep that the gradient is the main obstacle. Bar ends, low gearing, and energy are required! Day 3 has by far the most technical riding—slickrock and ledges show up frequently. Hardscrabble

Bottom offers differing challenges depending upon the conditions. The last day has a sandy theme. Seasoned sand riders will enjoy the riverside stroll while the rest grit their teeth and enjoy the scenery anyway. Horsethief Trail is steep but rates a moderate technically, as do the washboards back to the visitor center.

Trail surface: four-wheel-drive gravel road and paved road (avoidable with a shuttle). The four-wheel-drive road is mostly packed dirt. Some sections feature slickrock, ledges, clay, and sand. After Murphy's Hogback the road delivers more technical intricacies. Hardscrabble Bottom can be very soft if recently graded, extremely muddy and goopy if wet, and very rough if it has been wet, used, then dried and not yet graded. Actually the whole trail changes character when wet and may require chains for the sag vehicle! The Shafer and Horsethief Trails may be closed in wet weather.

Land status: Canyonlands National Park, Island in the Sky District. Permits are required for overnight use. The online reservation system is at canypermits.nps.gov/index.cfm.

Permits can be reserved as far as 4 months and at least 2 days in advance. The website shows available dates and campsites. Carefully read all of the National Park Service literature to be fully prepared. Regulations change; know and obey them. The maximum group size is 15 people with 3 vehicles.

Reservation help is available by phone Mon through Fri from 8 a.m. to 12:30 p.m. (mountain time) at (435) 259-4351 or via e-mail from nps.gov/cany/planyourvisit/backcountry permits.htm.

Maps: USGS Musselman Arch, Monument Basin, Turks Head, Upheaval Dome, Horsethief Canyon, Bowknot Bend, Mineral Canyon, The Knoll

Finding the trailhead: From Center and Main Streets in Moab, drive 11 miles north on US 191 to UT 313. Turn left and stay on the road all the way to the park gate. Continue about 0.5 mile past the visitor center to a parking area on the left. GPS: N38 27.627' / W109 49.235'. To avoid pedaling a long, washboarded stretch on the final day, leave a shuttle vehicle where Horsethief Trail tops out from Mineral Bottom. GPS: N38 30.519' / W109 59.752'. Drive 12.6 miles west on the access road that leaves from the west side of UT 313 about 8.9 miles north of the visitor center.

The Ride

0.0 From the parking area, turn right and pedal north toward the visitor center.

0.5 Visitor center. Be sure you've picked up your permit. Continue down the main road toward the park entrance gate.

1.5 Turn right onto the Shafer Trail. It's the dirt road on the right before you reach the park gate.

3.3 Brake check! The road drops away as it plunges toward the Colorado River.

6.8   The road forks. Keep right on the official White Rim Road. Left goes to the Shafer Campground and then to Potash Road.

8.1   The Goose Neck Trail (no bikes) goes left for an up close and personal view of its namesake and the Colorado River. It's a 0.7-mile round-trip hike.

9.8   The Walking Rocks Trail walks off to the left. This foot trail is a 0.4-mile round-trip.

10.0   Musselman Arch. Take pictures and walk the arch if you dare, but do not take your bike off the road or on the arch!

16.0   The top of a brief climb that separates the drainage of Little Bridge Canyon (behind) and Lathrop Canyon (ahead).

17.9   Lathrop Canyon foot trail leaves to the right en route to Island in the Sky. In 0.1 mile the day-use-only Lathrop Canyon Road leaves to the left and drops almost 500 feet in 3.5 miles down to the Colorado River.

18.8   Airport Tower campsites start here on the right. That big hunk of rock watching over this wide plateau is Airport Tower.

20.1   Washer Woman Rock slaves under the oppressive glare of Monster Tower where the road skirts the North Fork of Buck Canyon. The road then rounds Buck to continue past the Middle Fork and finally the South Fork at mile 27.

29.4   Gooseberry Trail heads up to Island in the Sky as the road rounds the point of Gooseberry Canyon. Campsites A and B lie just ahead on the left.

32.7   The pullout area for viewing Monument Basin comes up just after this rise. This is yet another wipe-off-the-chin view. There are more views into the basin through mile 36. Can you pick out the Totem Pole?

33.6   The road appears to fork, but tracks that lead down the wash on the right are from lost bikers. Do not follow them; keep left.

37.5 The road forks after this rise. The left-hand road leads 1.5 miles to White Crack Campsite on the point of the White Rim, a place worth visiting. One prohibitively sandy hill forces most riders to walk. White Crack has archaeological artifacts spread throughout the site. *Please leave them undisturbed.* Allow others to experience the same thrill of finding them (and preserve the site for further archaeological study). This is a nice campsite if you can secure it. To continue the main loop, go right at the fork, pedaling past Junction Butte above and on the right.

44.0 Time to pay for all the downhill. Cross the wash and start up the first pitch of Murphy's Hogback. This is only a warm-up for the final assault at mile 44.7. The southern branch of the Hogback trail leaves here for Island in the Sky.

45.1 The top of Murphy's Hogback delivers views of the entire planet and has three campsites. A rim-side seat from camp C gives vistas of Candlestick Tower (north-northwest), '50-Chevy Rock (north), and Soda Springs Basin (northwest). The north branch of the Hogback trail leaves from up here.

55.6 Candlestick Campsite. This camp works well on a four-night trip using Airport Towers, White Crack, Candlestick, and Labyrinth or Taylor Campsites.

57.9 After the most technical portion of trail so far, the Wilhite Trail heads right and up toward the Island. The wash crosses the road and enters a slot canyon. Confident friction climbers can dismount and follow it down to see its beauty from within. Farther down the road the Green River's Valentine Bottom comes into view.

62.1 An emergency water road leads down to Queen Anne's Bottom to the left. Keep bombing down the main road, and you won't even see it.

63.1 The road turns right, leaving lovely Queen Anne's Bottom behind and bearing toward Beaver Bottom. (I'm not making these names up, but apparently some lonely prospector did!)

66.0 The first of three Potato Bottom campsites. The next two are 0.6 and 0.7 mile farther, but all are in Potato Bottom Basin. ***Warning:*** Hardscrabble Hill lies dead ahead.

67.0 Up, up, and away. Hardscrabble Hill is here. Where's that 20-tooth front chainring when you need it?

68.2 Top. Don't go flying down the hill if you want to visit the ruins described at mile 68.6.

68.6 The road to the Fort Bottom trail goes left just after this corner. The road goes 0.5 mile to the foot trail, which leads another 1.2 miles to a ruin, thought to be Fremont, and an old cabin. The ruined tower is thought to be either defensive or ceremonial in purpose. The cabin was to be a stopping place for tuberculosis patients on their way to a never-built refuge near the confluence of the Colorado and Green Rivers.

70.3 The road turns right. Hardscrabble campsites are to the left.

71.6 The Syncline Valley foot trail through Upheaval Canyon to the Upheaval Dome goes right.

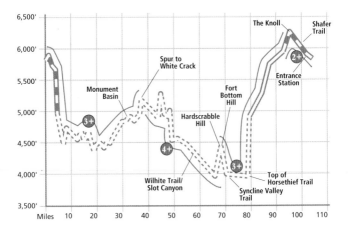

72.3 Keep left as the four-wheel-drive road to Taylor Campsite and Zeus and Moses Tower leaves to the right.

72.4 Labyrinth Campsite. The road ahead continues to be sandy and is now narrow. Sag drivers beware.

78.7 Turn right and head up to Horsethief Trail, which gains a gargantuan hunk of altitude in 1.5 miles. Left heads to Mineral Bottom.

80.2 Top. Look down on what you've accomplished!

80.3 This is where your shuttle vehicle should be parked. Otherwise ride this washboarded road back to the trailhead, avoiding all spurs.

92.9 Turn right on the paved road and follow it back to the park.

101.6 Visitor center.

103.1 Arrive back at the parking lot and trailhead. Hug your companions and revel in the conclusion of an odyssey while mourning its passing.

When thinking of these rocks one must not conceive of piles of boulders or heaps of fragments, but of a whole land of naked rock, with giant forms carved on it: cathedral-shaped buttes, towering hundreds or thousands of feet, cliffs that cannot be scaled, and canyon walls that shrink the river into insignificance, with vast, hollow domes and tall pinnacles and shafts set on the verge overhead; and all highly colored—buff, gray, red, brown, and chocolate—never lichened, never moss-covered, but bare, and often polished.

—JOHN WESLEY POWELL

Appendix A: The Kokopelli Trail

The Kokopelli is the original desert epic pieced together with old four-by-four roads and trails by the Colorado Plateau Mountain Bike Trail Association back in 1989. The eastern trailhead, near Fruita, Colorado, is a mountain-biking playground all by itself. It doesn't seem like riding from Fruita all the way to Moab is as popular as it once was. I suppose everyone is in a hurry and doesn't have the time for Kokopelli.

Why should you ride the Kokopelli? This is a bucket list adventure to tell the grandkids about. Although easier to supply than the White Rim Trail, it's tougher both technically and physically. Don't ride this on a whim. The trailheads are listed below. Permits aren't needed, but good planning is. Have a good riding partner and do more research than just reading this description. Entire books are written on this trail.

Location: From Loma, Colorado, to Moab

Distance: 142.0 miles point to point

Riding time: About 6 days (20-odd miles per day) with shuttle vehicles. Ordinary cars are sufficient for all but the final section, which requires a four-wheel-drive vehicle or described route adaptations to accommodate cars. With modern equipment and world-class legs, it's been done in less than 14 hours.

Physical difficulty: Strenuous. Ridden end to end, Kokopelli is long and the steeps are littered throughout.

Technical difficulty: Moderate to challenging. While there's plenty of spinning, the obstacles are numerous and diverse. And remote. The middle portions are mainly on dirt roads and aren't very technical.

Trail surface: 142 miles on every type of surface imaginable

Land status: Manti-La Sal National Forest, BLM Moab and Grand Junction Districts, and private holdings

Maps: USGS Mack, Ruby Canyon, Bitter Creek Well, Westwater, Agate, Big Triangle, Cisco, Dewey, Blue Chief Mesa, Fisher Valley, Mount Waas, Warner Lake, Rill Creek, Moab. The Grand Junction, Westwater, and Moab maps in the 1:100,000 series cover the route in a smaller scale and still show campsites. These maps may not have the new trail portions shown.

The Ride

Loma to Rabbit Valley—Section 1

Distance: 22 miles

Finding the trailhead: GPS: N39 10.667' / W108 49.671'

There are many options for riding from this trailhead. The Kokopelli is well blazed with brown fiberglass markers. Mary's Loop to Steve's Loop to Lion's Loop is the traditional route.

Campsite: Salt Creek Overlook

Rabbit Valley to Cisco—Section 2

Distance: 33 miles

Finding the trailhead: GPS: N39 11.106' / W109 00.987'

The trail leaves the trailhead westward and then turns left to head away from I-70.

Campsites: Rabbit, Castle Rock, Knowls Canyon Overlook, and Bitter Creek. Westwater is targeted for rafters.

Cisco to Dewey Bridge—Section 3

Distance: 21 miles

Finding the trailhead: GPS: N38 58.170' / W109 15.099'

The ride here is mainly gravel and sandy roads. A run along the Colorado River before crossing UT 128 offers up some fun.

Campsite: Fish Ford

Dewey Bridge to Onion Creek—Section 4

Distance: 18 miles

Finding the trailhead: GPS: N38 48.638' / W109 17.911'

The trail climbs up the gravel road that gets progressively rougher as it turns to a four-by-four road. *Don't follow* in a car past the trailhead to Ride 12.

Campsite: Cowskin

Across the Mesas—Section 5

Distance: 24 miles

Finding the trailhead: GPS: N38 41.333' / W109 13.230' or N38 36.714' / W109 11.745'

Major-league climbing here on gravel and paved roads. Nothing technically challenging.

Campsites: Hideout Canyon, Bull Draw

The Home Stretch—Section 6

Distance: 24 miles

Finding the trailhead: GPS: N38 35.735' / W109 17.418'

This isn't a trailhead but more of the section's start point. Many will combine section 5 and 6 when riding from east to west. There is no overnight parking at the visitor center. The trail follows the paved La Sal Loop Road and finishes off with the gravel Sand Flats Road. Options to take the Porcupine Rim (Ride 17) and its singletracks

(Ride 16) or a jaunt on the Slickrock Trail (Ride 1) exist for those wanting to end with some technically challenging riding.

Campsites: Sand Flats Recreation Area, Rock Castle, Mason Draw (aka Cold Springs)

Appendix B: Additional Rides

What? You want more?!

The region offers many more rides, some of which are best discovered by finding a local, earning his or her trust, and then getting invited along. But here are some rides for when such invites are hard to come by.

In the La Sals there are a couple of nice, steep rides that leave from the Pack Creek area. It's possible to make huge loops out of these four-wheel-drive roads or to link them to high-altitude singletrack. Access them by turning right about 2 miles past Ken's Lake on the Loop Road.

Heck, grab some maps and explore La Sal Pass Road and its evil twin to the north. Resurrect the Sheepherder's Loop or Bachelor's Bash. Also worth checking out are Lackey, Brumley, Dark Canyon Lake, Carpenter's Basin, and Black Ridge Roads. Black Ridge is directly across (east) from the trailhead of Rides 24 and 25.

The Canyon Rims Recreational Area, Canyonlands Needles District, and the Abajos Mountains near Monticello also have many more rides that didn't make this book. Lockhart Basin runs from Chicken Corners (Ride 23) to UT 211 in the Needles and makes a multiday trip with numerous side rides and hikes. This vast region to the south also includes the Seven Sisters Buttes, Aspen Flat, Shay Ridge, Elk Ridge, and Beef Basin rides. The Trout Water Canyon ride in the Canyon Rims Recreation Area hooks into the Boxcar Bridge route (Ride 35) for a nice loop. Flat Iron Mesa is a good roller with views of Kane Springs Canyon (Ride 26).

Adobe Mesa is a classic ride that is no longer in this book. It's the lesser-known sibling of Fisher Mesa (Ride 14). Follow the directions to Fisher Mesa. The trailhead is 2 miles closer than Fisher Mesa; 3.3 miles east of the La Sal Loop Road, down Castleton Road (GPS: N38 36.155' / W109 15.263').

Appendix C: Resources

Moab Information Center

Center and Main Street
Moab, UT 84532
(435) 259-8825 or (800) 635-MOAB (6622)
discovermoab.com
info2@discovermoab.com
This is the place to get almost any question answered. They may even know the meaning of life! The staff includes friendly folks from the National Park Service, Bureau of Land Management, and USDA Forest Service. Try here first.

Community Sand Flats Team

125 E. Center St.
Moab, UT 84532
(435) 259-2444
grandcountyutah.net
These folks are helping to restore and manage the area around the Slickrock Trail.

Trail Mix Grand County

www.grandcountyutah.net/trailmix
These are the folks with their names on all these new trails. Meetings are held at 182 N. 500 West (on 500 West between 400 North and Williams Way), in the northwest corner conference room, noon to 2 p.m. To receive copies of the agenda and minutes, please e-mail the secretary of the Grand County Council (council@grand.state.ut.us) and ask to be placed on the Trail Mix e-mail list.

Moab Trails Alliance

210 E. 300 South
Moab, UT 84532
http://moabtrails.wordpress.com
These folks raise money for trail projects.

Bureau of Land Management Moab District Office
82 E. Dogwood
P.O. Box 970
Moab, UT 84523
(435) 259-2100blm.gov

Grand County Travel Council
P.O. Box 550
Moab, UT 84532
(435) 259-8825 or (800) 635-6622 grandcounty utah.net

Canyonlands Natural History Association
3031 S. US Hwy. 191
Moab, UT 84532
(435) 259-6003cnha.org

Manti-La Sal National Forest
62 E. 100 North
Moab, UT 84532
(435) 259-7155
www.fs.usda.gov/ mantilasal

National Park Service—Canyonlands Information
Backcountry reservations:
(435) 259-4351
Information: (435) 719-2313nps.gov

Canyonlands National Park
Needles District Ranger Station
(435) 259-4711
www.nps.gov/cany

Arches National Park
P.O. Box 907
Moab, UT 84532
(435) 719-2299
www.nps.gov/arch

Dead Horse Point State Park
Camping reservations:
(800) 322-3770 or (435) 259-2614
www.stateparks.utah.gov

Utah Road Conditions and Weather Forecast
(801) 964-6000

Reservation Services
Moab/Canyonlands Central Reservations: (800) 748-4386
Infowest: (800) 576-2661
Camping information: (800) 635-6622

Appendix D: Showers

There comes a time when all riders must remove the deposits of trail and perspiration accumulated upon their persons. This act was once a major cause of friction between Moabites and bikers. The sinks in Moab are not there so bikers can prove how innovative they are at saving money. Think about the karma of the situation . . . before it breaks your chain in the middle of the desert.

The campgrounds and parks listed all charge a nominal fee for showers ranging from $4 to $8.

Archview Resort Campground—US 191 at UT 313, $6

Canyonlands Campground—555 S. Main St., $6

Dowd Flats RV Park—2701 S. US 191, $2.75 + 25 cents each 5 minutes

Lazy Lizard Hostel—1213 S. US 191, $3

Moab Cyclery—391 S. Main St., $5

Moab KOA—3255 S. US 191, $8

Moab Recreation and Aquatic Center—374 Park Ave., $4

Moab Rim RV Campark—1900 S. US 191, $5

OK RV Park—3310 Spanish Valley Rd., $5

Pack Creek Campground—1520 Murphy Ln., $4

Poison Spider Bicycles—497 N. Main St., $5 for 5 minutes ($1.50 per 2.5 minutes)

Riverside Oasis—1871 N. US 191, $5

Slickrock Campground—1301½ N. US 191, $4

Spanish Trail RV Park—2980 S. US 191, $5

Up the Creek Campground—210 E. 330 South, $6

Appendix E: Weather Info

Month	Sunrise	Sunset	High	Low	Precipitation
Jan	7:35	5:35	39.2	17.6	0.59
Feb	7:15	6:10	51.1	17.7	0.31
Mar	6:40	6:35	61.5	34.6	0.99
Apr	6:00	7:00	71.1	40.7	0.94
May	5:20	7:25	81.1	49.4	0.79
June	5:10	7:45	93.2	57.6	0.29
July	5:20	7:45	98.9	64.0	0.95
Aug	5:45	7:20	96.1	62.1	0.71
Sept	6:10	6:35	87.3	53.2	0.70
Oct	6:35	5:55	74.0	40.7	1.36
Nov	7:05	5:20	57.1	30.1	0.81
Dec	7:30	5:15	45.1	21.4	0.65

These are averages from twenty years' worth of data. Remember, an average is a number that corresponds to nothing in reality, but it does represent a point between the extremes. Temperatures can fluctuate dramatically in the desert!

Appendix F: Camping

Once upon a time camping was free in a number of areas around Moab. The Colorado River corridor, Kane Springs, Ken's Lake, Behind the Rocks, and Sand Flats suffered from hoards of people who had no respect for the outdoors. Now these areas are regulated. This means it costs to camp around Moab. If you're not paying someone, chances are you're in the wrong place.

The Bureau of Land Management (BLM) now charges a small fee of $5 for rustic site camping along the Colorado River (UT 128). The self-pay sites are marked with a tent icon on brown posts and are open all year. These sites are among a few closed sites marked with the same icon with a red circle and a slash over it. Don't even think of camping in a closed spot. For more information, contact Bureau of Land Management, Moab District Office, 82 E. Dogwood, P.O. Box 970, Moab, UT 84523; (435) 259-2100; www.blm.gov.

BLM Campgrounds on UT 128 (River Road)

Goose Island—18 sites 1.4 miles from US 191

Granstaff—16 sites 3 miles from US 191

Drinks Canyon—17 sites 6.2 miles from US 191

Hal Canyon—11 sites 6.6 miles from US 191

Oak Grove—7 sites 6.9 miles from US 191

Big Bend—23 sites 7.4 miles from US 191

Upper Big Bend—8 sites 8.1 miles from US 191

Lower Onion Creek—4 sites 21.5 miles from US 191, dirt road access

Fisher Tower—5 sites 21.5 miles from US 191, dirt road access

Hittle Bottom—10 sites 22.5 miles from US 191

Dewey Bridge—7 sites 29 miles from US 191

While camping along UT 128, you may see strange lights illuminating the canyon walls and voices echoing down the canyon. This is only the nightly tour that floats down the river complete with PA system and spotlight-equipped support vehicles.

If your camp area doesn't have a trash bin, pack out your trash to neighboring Goose Island and Big Bend campsites.

BLM Campgrounds on UT 279 (near Rides 31 and 33)

Jay Cee Park—7 sites 4 miles west of US 191
Williams Bottom—17 sites 6 miles from US 191
GoldBar—5 sites 10 miles west of US 191

BLM Campgrounds on Kane Creek Boulevard

Kings Bottom—11 sites 2.8 miles west of US 191
MoonFlower—8 sites 3 miles west of US 191
Hunters Canyon—13 sites 7.8 miles west of US 191 (on dirt road)
The Ledge—18 sites 10 miles from US 191

Other Area BLM Campgrounds

Sand Flats Recreation Area—143 sites 2 miles east of Moab (see appendix G)
Ken's Lake—31 sites 8.5 miles from US 191 (see access directions for Ride 27, Flat Pass)
Horsethief—56 sites 12 miles from US 191 off UT 313
Cowboy Camp—7 sites 14 miles from US 191 off UT 313

Other Nonprivate Campgrounds
La Sal National Forest

Warner Lake Campground—22 seasonal sites on La Sal Loop Road (in mountains) 24 miles from Moab
Oowah Campground—8 seasonal sites
Mason Draw Campground—5 seasonal sites

Arches National Park
Devils Garden—53 sites

Canyonlands National Park
Needles District—26 sites
Island in the Sky District—12 sites

Dead Horse Point State Park
21 RV sites 31 miles from Moab on UT 313

Private Campgrounds
Archview Resort Campground—US 191 at UT 313; (435) 259-7854 (seasonal) or (800) 813-6622; dump station and water available for a fee

Ballard RV Park—100 S. Main, Thompson Springs, UT (865) 250-8061

Base Camp—Near Jackson Hole on the Colorado River; 1010 Hurrah Pass Rd.; (435) 258-6264 (Skype), (435) 260-1783 (cell if in range)

Canyonlands Campground—555 S. Main St.; (435) 259-6848 or (800) 522-6848; dump station and water available for a fee

Dowd Flats RV Park—2701 South US 191; (435) 259-5909

Lions Back Camp Park—Sand Flats Road west of Sand Flats Recreation Area; (435) 259-7954

Moab KOA—3225 S. US 191; (435) 259-6682 (seasonal) or (800) 562-0372

Moab Rim Campark—1900 S. US 191; (435) 259-5002 (seasonal) or (888) 599-6622

Moab Valley RV & Campark—1773 S. US 191; (435) 259-4469 (seasonal)

OK RV Park & Canyonlands Stables—3310 Spanish Valley Rd.; (435) 259-1400; dump station and water available for a fee

Pack Creek Campground—1520 Murphy Lane, #6; (435) 259-2982

Portal RV Park & Fishery—1261 N. US 191; (435) 259-6108 or (800) 574-2028

Riverside Oasis—1861 N. US 191; (435) 259-3424 (seasonal) or (877) 285-7757

Slickrock Campground—1301½ N. US 191; (435) 259-7660 or (800) 448-8873; dump station and water available for a fee

Spanish Trail RV Park—2980 S. US 191; (435) 259-2411 (seasonal) or (800) 787-2751

Up the Creek—210 E. 300 South in Moab; (435) 259-6995 (seasonal)

RV Dump Station

Farm & City General Store—850 S. Main St.; (435) 259-0169; dump station and water available for a fee

Appendix G:
Sand Flats Recreational Area

To access Slickrock Trail (Ride 1) and Porcupine Rim (Ride 17) or camp along Sand Flats Road, you must pay a fee. If there isn't anyone in the entrance house, use the self-pay station.

Before you grumble too much about this, you should know how bad the area was becoming before fees were charged. The anarchy that was Sand Flats wasn't good for the land. Now the area is managed by the Community Sand Flats Team, and things are looking good. Besides, the fees are extremely low.

Passes are sold by the day ($5 per vehicle or $2 per biker if you ride in). If you take a shuttle in, you still owe the fee at the gate though the shuttle driver may have already charged you (find out). The pass (your receipt) is good for the day. Want more? You can also purchase a weeklong or annual pass for $10 or $20 respectively.

At the entrance gate is a message board and information kiosk. Keep in mind that cell service is very spotty out here. This is a great place to meet up with fellow bikers. By the way, another such message board is at Eddie McStiff's, next to the Moab Information Center.

There are 143 campsites at Sand Flats. The fee for each site is $10 per vehicle, which covers five people; there's a small extra fee of $2 per additional person. Group sites for sixteen to twenty people are available for $50 to $60 per night and a one-time $10 reservation fee. Campers have a checkout time of 1 p.m. As a courtesy to other campers, a 10 p.m. to 6 a.m. quiet time is in effect. The sites are in clusters that have toilets but no trash bins. Trash should be packed out or placed in the bins located at the Slickrock Trailhead.

There is absolutely no gathering or cutting of firewood or tinder. That gnarled juniper log is part of the desert environment. Fires are allowed in the metal fire rings with wood you brought with you. Firewood is available in town at City Market or most gas stations/convenience stores. Walkers Hardware, among others, has propane for your camp stove.

Appendix H: Bike Shop Heaven

Moab probably has more bike shops per capita than anywhere else on the planet, so it is well equipped to handle all a biker needs. While the area's population is around 8,000, Moab offers more biking amenities than most big cities. At last count, seven bike shops carry everything from patches to full-suspension, high-dollar, custom rigs. What this means in the real world is good service and competitive prices. It also means lots of good advice on equipment, rental rigs, trail updates, tours, and shuttle information. Each shop has its own feel, and some even have espresso!

Chile Pepper Bike Shop
702 S. Main St.
Moab, UT 84532
(435) 259-4688 or (888) 677-4688
chilebikes.com

Moab Cyclery
391 S. Main St.
Moab, UT 84532
(435) 259-7423 or (800) 559-1978 moabcyclery.com

Poison Spider Bicycles
497 N. Main St.
Moab, UT 84532
(435) 259-7882 or (800) 635-1792
poisonspiderbicycles.com

Rim Cyclery
94 W. 100 N.
Moab, UT 84532
(435) 259-5333 or (888) 304-8219 rimcyclery.com

Appendix I: Trailhead Shuttles

"It's a dangerous business, Frodo, going out your door.
You step onto the road, and if you don't keep your feet,
there's no knowing where you might be swept off to."
—THE LORD OF THE RINGS, J.R.R. TOLKIEN

Chile Pepper Bike Shop—(435) 259-4688 or
(888) 677-4688

Coyote Shuttle—(435) 260-2097

DirtSeeker—(435) 259-2213

Moab Cyclery/Escape Adventures—(435) 259-7423
or (800) 559-1978

Moab Luxury Coach—(435) 940-4212 or
(855) 456-8824

Moab Tour Company—(435) 259-4080 or
(877) 725-7317

NAVTEC Expeditions—(435) 259-7983 or
(800) 833-1278

Porcupine Shuttle—(435) 260-0896

Roadrunner Shuttle—(435) 259-9402

Whole Enchilada Shuttles—(435) 260-2534

Appendix J:
Mountain-Biking Guidelines

If every mountain biker always yielded the right-of-way, stayed on the trail, avoided wet or muddy trails, rode in control, showed respect for other trail users, carried out every last scrap of what was carried in (candy wrappers and bike-part debris included), and never cut switchbacks—in short, if we all did the right things—we wouldn't need a list of rules governing our behavior.

The fact is most mountain bikers are conscientious and try to do the right thing; however, thousands of miles of dirt trails have been closed due to the irresponsible habits of a few riders.

Here are some basic guidelines adapted from the International Mountain Bicycling Association (IMBA) Rules of the Trail. These guidelines can help prevent damage to land, water, plants, and wildlife; maintain trail access; and avoid conflicts with other backcountry visitors and trail users. Here's a basic rule of thumb: Don't make a trail around an obstacle, and be courteous to others.

1. Only ride on trails that are open. Don't trespass on private land, and be sure to obtain any necessary permits. If you're not sure if a trail is closed or if you need a permit, don't hesitate to ask.

2. Keep your bicycle under control. Watch the condition of the trail at all times, and follow the appropriate speed regulations and recommendations.

3. Yield to others on the trail. Make your approach well known in advance, either with a friendly greeting or a bell. When approaching a corner, junction, or blind spot, expect to encounter other trail users.

When passing others, show your respect by slowing to a walking pace.

4. Don't startle animals. Animals may be easily scared by sudden approaches or loud noises. For your safety—and the safety of others in the area as well as the animals themselves—give all wildlife a wide berth. When encountering horses, defer to the horseback riders' directions.

5. Have zero impact. Be aware of the impact you're making on the trail beneath you. You should not ride under conditions where you will leave evidence of your passing, such as on certain soils after rain. If a ride features optional side hikes into wilderness areas, be a zero-impact hiker too. Whether you're on bike or on foot, stick to existing trails, leave gates as you found them, and carry out everything you brought in.

6. Be prepared. Know the equipment you are using, the area where you'll be riding, and your cycling abilities and limitations. Avoid unnecessary breakdowns by keeping your equipment in good shape. When you head out, bring spare parts and supplies for weather changes. Be sure to wear appropriate safety gear, including a helmet, and learn how to be self-sufficient.

About the Author

Well, here I am at the end of an update to a book I first wrote in 1995. Back then I wrote the "About the Author" section and continued a story of my life that I'd started in *Fattracks Colorado Springs* (now *Mountain Biking Colorado Springs*).

I told of my love for the outdoors and riding BMX bikes on mountain trails near my tiny hometown of West-cliffe, Colorado.

I told of my BS degree in Psychology (go Rams) and being a private investigator and a ski-mountain photographer (possibly the best job ever). I wondered if I'd return to Colorado after leaving for California.

Then came the Moab book. I jumped at the chance and moved to Moab. I had been living in Ventura, California, where I was surfing every day. My custom longboard was still new. Now it's yellowed and ready to be hung on the wall as art.

I waxed poetic about Mother Earth and Moab. ". . . Moab inspires that same oneness with the Earth. The rocks here show the Earth's patience and strength. It's a patience that society seems to eat away at with its deadlines and daytimers."

Now, eighteen years later and thanks to Moab's singletrack revival, I've had the chance to spend as much time updating this guide as I did writing it in the first place. Moab has "returned" to its rightful place atop the mountain-biking realm. Yet Moab never really left. Maybe people forgot and needed a reason to rediscover it.

I think I've changed just as much. I'm living in Oceanside, California, with my wife, Heidi, and my two awesome kids, Dawson and Amber. As I mentioned in the acknowledgments, the whole family helped update the book. I spend three days a week as a home educator for my kids' charter school. At times it seems everything has changed.

Or has it? I still find myself outside with a desire to share the fun with others, whether it's riding my bike so I can share Moab's trails with you or standing on a baseball diamond surrounded by 9- to 11-year-olds sharing the joys of baseball and Little League.

That old "About the Author" written in 1995 said the main thing to know about me is that I enjoy life. That is still the case, with one addendum. Now I know that it just keeps getting better!

I hope this guide helps you experience a bit of Moab and its enchanted surroundings while showing respect for our Earth.

Enjoy!
—Dave

INTERNATIONAL MOUNTAIN
BICYCLING ASSOCIATION

Come Ride With Us!

You've just purchased, or are about to purchase, the mountain bike of your dreams. Where will you take your new steed? Who will you ride with? Joining IMBA's network of chapters, clubs and patrols taps you into a friendly network of experienced mountain bikers. They host rides for all skill levels, build trails and get together before and after rides to share stories and plan the next adventure. Find a local group by visiting imba.com/near-you.

FIVE RECENT ACCOMPLISHMENTS

1) **Built incredible trails.** IMBA's trailbuilding pros teamed with volunteers around the nation to build sustainable, fun singletrack like the 32-mile system at Pennsylvania's Raystown Lake.

2) **Won grants to build or improve trails.** Your contributions to IMBA's Trail Building Fund were multiplied with six-figure grants of federal money for trail systems.

3) **Challenged anti-bike policies.** IMBA works closely with all of the federal land managing agencies and advises them on how to create bike opportunities and avoid policies that curtail trail access.

4) **Made your voice heard.** When anti-bike interests moved to try to close sections of the 2,500-mile Continental Divide trail to bikes, IMBA rallied its members and collected more than 7,000 comments supporting keeping the trail open to bikes.

5) **Put kids on bikes.** The seventh edition of National Take a Kid Mountain Biking Day put more than 20,000 children on bikes.

FIVE CURRENT GOALS

1) **Host regional bike summits.** We're boosting local trail development by hosting summits in distinct regions of the country, bringing trail advocates and regional land managers together.

2) **Build the next generation of trail systems** with innovative projects, including IMBA's sustainably built "flow trails" for gravity-assisted fun!

3) **Create "Gateway" trails** to bring new riders into the sport.

4) **Fight blanket bans against bikes** that unwisely suggest we don't belong in backcountry places.

5) **Strengthen its network** of IMBA-affiliated clubs with a powerful chapter program.

FOUR THINGS YOU CAN
DO FOR YOUR SPORT

1) **Join IMBA.** Get involved with IMBA and take action close to home through your local IMBA-affiliated club. An organization is only as strong as its grassroots membership. IMBA needs your help in protecting and building great trails right here.

2) **Volunteer.** Join a trail crew day for the immensely satisfying experience of building a trail you'll ride for years to come. Ask us how.

3) **Speak up.** Tell land-use and elected officials how important it is to preserve mountain bike access. Visit IMBA's web site for action issues and talking points.

4) **Respect other trail users.** Bike bans result from conflict, real or perceived. By being good trail citizens, we can help end the argument that we don't belong on trails.

YOU BELONG WITH IMBA

JOIN

Join IMBA at www.imba.com or call 1-888-442-IMBA